STAR WARS™

CHARACTER ENCYCLOPEDIA

UPDATED AND EXPANDED

WRITTEN BY
**SIMON BEECROFT, ELIZABETH DOWSETT,
AND PABLO HIDALGO**

CONTENTS

Who stole the Death Star plans? Which droid became a ruthless bounty hunter? Who can breathe on land and underwater? The galaxy is full of heroes, villains, aliens, creatures, and droids. All have played a part—large or small—in the events of the dying days of the Galactic Republic, the battles of the Clone Wars, the desperate rebellion against the Empire, and the rise of the First Order.

FINDING A CHARACTER

Look up characters alphabetically by their first name or title, or use the index on page 222.

2-1B

SURGICAL DROID

Vocabulator

Transparent
shell over
hydraulics

DATA FILE

AFFILIATION: None
TYPE: Surgical droid
MANUFACTURER:
Industrial Automaton
HEIGHT: 1.77m (5ft 8in)
APPEARANCES: III, V,
VI, S
SEE ALSO: Darth Vader;
Luke Skywalker

2-1B MEDICAL and surgical droids have been around since Republic times. One such unit is attached to the rebel base on Hoth. He treats the injuries of many rebel troops, including Luke Skywalker after a wampa attacks him.

SURGICAL DROIDS in the 2-1B
series are equipped with encyclopedic memory banks. They ensure that the droids give the best course of treatment in any medical situation.

Hydraulic leg

A Republic-era 2-1B droid rebuilds Darth Vader's burned body.

Rebel Surgeon

2-1B is able to perform extremely precise operations that leave little or no scar. The droid's long experience with humans makes him a caring medic. Luke Skywalker is so impressed with 2-1B's skills, he requests that the droid treats him again after he loses his hand on Cloud City.

Stabilizing foot

4-LOM

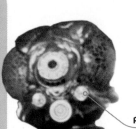

DATA FILE

AFFILIATION: Bounty hunter

TYPE: LOM-series protocol droid

MANUFACTURER: Industrial Automaton

HEIGHT: 1.67m (5ft 5in)

APPEARANCES: V

SEE ALSO: Darth Vader; Jabba the Hutt; Zuckuss

Compound photoreceptors

BlasTech DLT-19 heavy blaster rifle

Battered black droid plating

After the Battle of Hoth, Vader hires 4-LOM and others to locate the *Millennium Falcon*.

THIS HUMANOID DROID with an insect-like face used to be a sophisticated protocol droid made to resemble the species he served. 4-LOM was once assigned to a luxury liner, but he overwrote his own programming and began a life of crime as a bounty hunter.

THE PERSONALITY

software corruption that transformed 4-LOM into a deadly bounty hunter is a known flaw in the LOM-series. Other similarly affected protocol droids of the same make have been spotted working as enforcers in the Outer Rim Territories.

Dangerous Duo

4-LOM often works in partnership with a bounty hunter named Zuckuss. The combination of 4-LOM's powers of deduction and analysis with Zuckuss's mystical intuition makes their collaboration successful and lucrative.

AAYLA SECURA

TWI'LEK JEDI KNIGHT

DATA FILE

AFFILIATION: Jedi
HOMEWORLD: Ryloth
SPECIES: Twi'lek
HEIGHT: 1.7m (5ft 6in)
APPEARANCES: II, III
SEE ALSO: Kit Fisto; Mace
Windu; Yoda

Lekku
(head-tail)

Lightsaber
powered by a blue
kyber crystal

CUNNING AAYLA SECURA

is a Twi'lek Jedi Knight who
relies on her athletic lightsaber
skills to outwit opponents.
As a Jedi General, Aayla
leads a squad of clone
troopers on many campaigns.

AAYLA SECURA is an
intelligent, sometimes mischievous
Jedi. Her teacher was a troubled Jedi
named Quinlan Vos. Aayla passes
on the teachings of her Master to
young Ahsoka Tano during a
Clone Wars mission that goes
awry, and ends up on the
grassland planet of Maridun.

Belt made
of rycrit hide

Fitted clothing allows
complete freedom of
movement

Secura's own clone troopers
turn on her on Felucia.

Captured

At the Battle of Geonosis, Aayla Secura
is among the circle of Jedi captured
by Geonosian soldiers. Luckily,
clone trooper reinforcements
come to their rescue.

ADI GALLIA

THOLOTHIAN JEDI MASTER

DATA FILE

AFFILIATION: Jedi
HOMEWORLD: Coruscant
SPECIES: Tholothian
HEIGHT: 1.84m (6ft)
APPEARANCES: I, II
SEE ALSO: Bail Organa;
Chancellor Valorum; Even
Piell; Stass Allie

JEDI MASTER ADI GALLIA was born into a high-ranking diplomatic family stationed on Coruscant. Gallia is a Jedi High Council member and a noble General in the Clone Wars.

Long, fleshy tendrils descend from scaled cranium

Jedi robe

Lightsaber

Utility pouch

As a High Council member, Adi Gallia is respected for her powers of intuition.

Tall travel boots

ADI GALLIA was a valuable intelligence source to Senate leaders. Her life was cut short in the Clone Wars when she was killed by the renegade Sith apprentice Savage Opress.

Jedi Temple

Gallia may be stationed at the Jedi Temple on Coruscant, but she is finely attuned to events further afield. Gallia is the first to warn the Senate of the Trade Federation's suspicious activity in the Naboo System.

ADMIRAL ACKBAR

RESISTANCE SPACE FORCE ADMIRAL

DATA FILE

AFFILIATION: Rebel Alliance/ Resistance
HOMEWORLD: Mon Cala
SPECIES: Mon Calamari
HEIGHT: 1.8m (5ft 9in)
APPEARANCES: VI, VII, VIII
SEE ALSO: General Madine; Mon Mothma; Princess Leia

ADMIRAL ACKBAR was born on the ocean world of Mon Cala. A veteran of the Clone Wars, he is later instrumental in bringing his people into the Rebel Alliance. After the Galactic Civil War, he is coaxed out of retirement by Princess Leia to join the Resistance during the rise of the First Order.

Rank badge

Waterproof skin

Belt clasp

Ackbar commanded the rebel fleet from his personal flagship, *Home One*.

AS COMMANDER

of the rebel fleet, Admiral Ackbar planned and led the attack on the Empire's capital ships at the Battle of Endor.

Many years after the civil war, Ackbar serves as part of the Resistance command staff at the base on D'Qar.

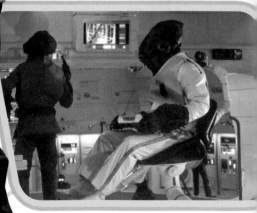

Home One

Ackbar's people contributed their giant Mon Cal star cruisers to the Alliance. *Home One* served as a mobile command center after the Empire discovered and destroyed the main Alliance headquarters on Hoth.

ADMIRAL OZZEL

ADMIRAL OF THE *EXECUTOR*

AFFILIATION: Empire
HOMEWORLD: Carida
SPECIES: Human
HEIGHT: 1.75m (5ft 7in)
APPEARANCES: V
SEE ALSO: Admiral Piett;
General Veers; Darth Vader

Officer's disk

KENDAL OZZEL is the commander of Darth Vader's gigantic flagship, the *Executor*. Under Ozzel's sometimes uncertain command, the *Executor* emerges from hyperspace too close to Hoth, alerting the rebels to the Imperials' presence.

Imperial code cylinder

Rank insignia plaque

Belt buckle contains secret data-storage compartment

KENDAL OZZEL
serves in the Republic Navy during the Clone Wars and soon works his way up the military ladder. Ozzel is ambitious but displays poor judgment and ineffective tactical thinking, which he attempts to mask with his authoritarian persona.

The *Executor* leads Darth Vader's personal fleet of Star Destroyers, known as the Death Squadron.

Deadly Blunders

Vader's view of Ozzel is that he is "as clumsy as he is stupid." After a series of blunders by Ozzel—first, doubting evidence of life on Hoth, then the failed attempt to surprise the rebels—Vader Force-chokes Ozzel and promotes Captain Piett to Admiral in Ozzel's place.

Durasteel-toed boots

ADMIRAL PIETT

COMMANDER OF THE *EXECUTOR*

DATA FILE

AFFILIATION: Empire
HOMEWORLD: Axxila
SPECIES: Human
HEIGHT: 1.73m (5ft 7in)
APPEARANCES: V, VI
SEE ALSO: Admiral Ozzel;
Darth Vader

An A-wing destroys the
Executor's bridge crew and
causes the ship to crash.

Naval
officer's
tunic

PIETT IS A LOYAL IMPERIAL captain on Darth Vader's flagship, the *Executor*. After Vader Force-chokes Admiral Ozzel to death for incompetence, Piett is instantly promoted to admiral of the fleet. Piett loses his life when a rebel A-wing crashes through the bridge of the *Executor*.

Leather gloves

UNLIKE MOST Imperial officers, who come from the prestigious Inner Core worlds, Firmus Piett has his origins in the Outer Rim. He is known for his quick thinking, as well as his ability to shift blame for mistakes he has made.

Risky Strategy

Vader's officers must submit entirely to the Dark Lord's iron will. When Vader insists that Piett makes a risky pursuit of the *Millennium Falcon* into an asteroid field, Piett nervously does Vader's bidding, aware that errors could lead to his death.

ADMIRAL RADDUS

MON CALAMARI COMMANDER OF THE FLEET

DATA FILE

AFFILIATION: Rebel Alliance
HOMEWORLD: Mon Cala
SPECIES: Mon Calamari
HEIGHT: 1.9m (6ft 2in)
APPEARANCES: RO
SEE ALSO: Admiral Ackbar; General Merrick; Princess Leia

Fishlike eyes see well on land and under water

ADMIRAL RADDUS was an early recruit to the Rebel cause when the Empire overran his aquatic homeworld, Mon Cala. Stern and steely, Raddus makes a determined and dedicated fleet commander.

Mon Cala civic crest awarded for planetary defense

Waterproof datapad with orders

RADDUS HAS

experience of city defense and leadership skills he honed as Mayor of Nystullum. He also gives the fledgling Alliance fleet the *Profundity*, a city-ship, now converted into a warship.

Raddus is not one to shy from battle. When he hears of the rogue Scarif mission, he leaps to their support.

Honored Hero

Raddus's direct and pragmatic manner does not endear him to everyone. But such is his contribution and sacrifice to the rebel cause, many years later, General Organa's Star Cruiser is named the *Raddus*, in his honor.

ADMIRAL STATURA

RESISTANCE OFFICER

DATA FILE

AFFILIATION: Resistance
HOMEWORLD: Garel
SPECIES: Human
HEIGHT: 1.72m (5ft 6in)
APPEARANCES: VII
SEE ALSO: Admiral Ackbar; General Ematt; Major Brance; Princess Leia

STATURA WAS ONLY a teenager when the war against the Galactic Empire ended, but he experienced combat firsthand while trying to liberate his homeworld from Imperial rule. He loyally serves General Leia Organa.

Repurposed Rebel Alliance crest

Admiral's rank badge

WHEN GENERAL Organa assembled trusted military advisors to form the core of her Resistance movement, she turned to experienced rebel veterans. Statura was younger than most, and plucked from a career in applied sciences.

Statura watches the battle above the Starkiller unfold from the Resistance command center on D'Qar.

Battle Analysis

Statura is practical and technically minded, traits he uses well in his role supervising logistics for the Resistance. He keenly assesses the Starkiller threat, correctly guessing the unimaginable scale of its destructive power. It is his analysis that leads to the Resistance starfighter attack on the weapon.

AGEN KOLAR

ZABRAK JEDI MASTER

DATA FILE

AFFILIATION: Jedi
HOMEWORLD: Coruscant
SPECIES: Zabrak
HEIGHT: 1.9m (6ft 2in)
APPEARANCES: II, III
SEE ALSO: Kit Fisto;
Mace Windu; Saesee Tiin

Horns
regenerate
over time

Lightsaber uses dual
crystals to create green
or blue energy blades

Two-handed
ready stance

AGEN KOLAR is
a master swordsmith
who joins the 200 Jedi
Knights that battle the
Separatist Army on
Geonosis. Mace Windu
has a high opinion of
Kolar's combat skills,
and enlists him in a
desperate attempt
to arrest Supreme
Chancellor Palpatine.

AGEN KOLAR is a
Zabrak, as is fellow Jedi Eeth
Koth. The Zabrak species is
identified by its head horns.
Known to strike first and ask
questions later, Kolar is also
a valuable member of the
Jedi High Council.

Hooded robe often
removed in combat

Agen Kolar's renowned lightsaber
skills are put to use on Geonosis.

Skillful Sith

Even the celebrated sword skills
of Agen Kolar cannot match the
speed and unsparing power of
a Sith Lord such as Darth Sidious.

ANAKIN SKYWALKER

LEGENDARY JEDI KNIGHT

Gauntlet covers mechno-hand (which replaces hand sliced off by Count Dooku)

DATA FILE

AFFILIATION: Podracing, Jedi, Sith
HOMEWORLD: Tatooine
SPECIES: Human
HEIGHT: 1.85m (6ft 1in)
APPEARANCES: I, II, III, VI
SEE ALSO: Obi-Wan Kenobi; Padmé Amidala; Qui-Gon Jinn

Jedi utility belt

Young Anakin's keen perception and unnaturally fast reflexes show his great Force potential.

IN THE CLONE WARS,
Anakin loses his faith in the Jedi to restore peace and harmony to the galaxy. He also feels great anger at the tragic death of his mother and fears that the same fate may befall Padmé Amidala (who is secretly his wife). Finally, Anakin is persuaded that only the dark side can give him the power to prevent death.

ANAKIN SKYWALKER'S
rise to power is astonishing. In a few short years, he goes from being a slave on Tatooine to becoming one of the most powerful Jedi ever. But Anakin's thirst for power leads him to the dark side of the Force, with tragic consequences for the galaxy.

Close Bond
Anakin's bond with his teacher, Obi-Wan Kenobi, is strong. They make a dynamic team in the Clone Wars, where Anakin proves to be a great leader. Yet Anakin is troubled by feelings of anger and mistrust.

Anakin's impulsive nature leads him toward the dark side.

14

AT-AT PILOT

IMPERIAL WALKER OPERATORS

ONLY THE STRONGEST Imperial soldiers are put forward for training to become pilots of the terrifying All Terrain Armored Transport (AT-AT) walkers. AT-AT pilots, who generally work in pairs, consider themselves all-powerful.

Reinforced helmet

Life-support pack

Insulated jumpsuit

AT-ATs are not climate controlled, so pilots wear special insulated suits on frozen planets such as Hoth. The suits protect the wearer if the walker's pressurized cockpit is smashed open in hostile environments.

Driving gauntlet

The pilots sit in the cockpit in the AT-AT's head, operating driving and firing controls.

Walking Terror

The giant AT-AT walkers march relentlessly across uneven battlegrounds, using their mighty laser cannons to wreak destruction on the enemy forces below.

AT-ST PILOT

IMPERIAL SCOUT WALKER CREW

DATA FILE

AFFILIATION: Empire
SPECIES: Human
STANDARD EQUIPMENT:
Blasters; grenades; thermal
detonators; emergency
flares; comlink
APPEARANCES: V, VI
SEE ALSO: AT-AT pilot;
Chewbacca

AT-STs are equipped with two
powerful medium blaster cannons.

Jumpsuit

AT-ST PILOTS wear
open-face helmets, blast goggles,
and basic armor plating under their
jumpsuits. In the Battle of Endor,
AT-ST walkers are deployed against
the rebels. Many are lost to surprise
attacks by Ewoks.

TWO-LEGGED AT-ST

(All Terrain Scout
Transport) walkers march
into battle, spraying
blaster bolts at enemy
troops. Each walker
houses two highly trained
pilots with superior skills
of balance and agility.

Fire-resistant
gauntlet

Two pilots keep the AT-ST
walker moving at speed
through uneven terrain.

On the Hunt

AT-ST walkers are used on reconnaissance
and anti-personnel hunting missions.
They are not invulnerable to attack, as
Chewbacca demonstrates when he forces
his way inside a walker through the roof.

AURRA SING

DATA FILE

AFFILIATION: Bounty hunter
HOMEWORLD: Nar Shaddaa
SPECIES: Human
HEIGHT: 1.83m (6ft)
APPEARANCES: I
SEE ALSO: Boba Fett; Bossk;
Padmé Amidala

AURRA SING is a ruthless bounty hunter. A seemingly ageless veteran of the underworld scene, Aurra worked with such contemporaries as Jango Fett and Cad Bane. During the Clone Wars, she was hired by Ziro the Hutt to assassinate Padmé Amidala.

Tracker utility vest

Short-range pistol

Long fingers to draw blood

AURRA SING was born in the polluted urban sprawl of Nar Shaddaa. She never knew her father and her mother was too poor to raise her. Sing became a cold-blooded killer. She is willing to use any means necessary to locate her prey. She has sensor implants and has a wide assortment of weapons in her private arsenal, including lightsabers and a sniper's projectile rifle.

Long-range projectile rifle

During the Clone Wars, Aurra guides the recently orphaned Boba Fett.

High Alert

On the trail of her quarry on Tatooine, Aurra Sing is a spectator at the podrace that will earn young Anakin Skywalker his freedom.

A-WING PILOT

DATA FILE

AFFILIATION: Rebel Alliance
SQUADRON NAMES: Phoenix Squadron, Green Group
SQUADRON LEADERS: Hera Syndulla (Phoenix Leader); Arvel Crynyd (Green Leader)
APPEARANCES: VI
SEE ALSO: Admiral Ackbar; Lando Calrissian

Comlink helps pilots communicate during missions

Flak vest

Pressurized g-suit

Data cylinders

Gear harness

A-WINGS ARE small, super-fast starfighters and A-wing pilots are some of the most talented fliers in the Rebel Alliance. These pilots play a pivotal role at the Battle of Endor when they destroy Vader's ship, the *Executor*.

Rebel pilot Arvel Crynyd pilots his damaged A-wing into the bridge of the *Executor*.

A-WING starfighters started serving the Rebellion before the Battle of Yavin. Earlier versions of the craft were the mainstay vessels of Phoenix Squadron, a rebel cell operating in and around the Lothal sector in the Outer Rim Territories.

Capable Ships

Only the very best rebel pilots can fly the powerful A-wings. Originally designed as an escort ship, the A-wing's incredible speed and maneuverability make it a deadly strike craft. A-wings also use concealed sensors to gather information on Imperial ships.

BAIL ORGANA

VICEROY OF ALDERAAN

DATA FILE

AFFILIATION:
Republic/Rebel Alliance
HOMEWORLD: Alderaan
SPECIES: Human
HEIGHT: 1.91m (6ft 3in)
APPEARANCES: II, III, RO
SEE ALSO: Mon Mothma; Princess Leia

Alderaanian cloak

Target blaster

Action boots

Bail and his wife, Breha, adopt Leia after Padmé's death.

BAIL ORGANA is the Senator for Alderaan. He watches, horrified, as the Galactic Republic becomes a dictatorship under Palpatine. Along with Mon Mothma, Bail is one of the founders of the Rebellion against Emperor Palpatine.

Alderaanian belt

ORGANA remains loyal to the Republic and the Jedi Order to the end. In Imperial times, it is Bail who responds to the threat of the Death Star by sending his adopted daughter, Leia, on a mission to locate Obi-Wan Kenobi in order to recruit him to the Rebel Alliance.

After Order 66, Bail assists any survivors that he can.

Influential Contact

When the rebels learn of the Death Star threat, Mon Mothma turns to Bail for help. An old friend of his is a Jedi in hiding, and Bail's daughter, Princess Leia, might be able to track him down.

BALA-TIK

GUAVIAN FRONTMAN

DATA FILE

AFFILIATION: Guavian Death Gang
HOMEWORLD: Unknown
SPECIES: Human
HEIGHT: 1.8m (5ft 9in)
APPEARANCES: VII
SEE ALSO: Guavian Security Soldier; Han Solo; Kanjiklub gang; Tasu Leech

AN AGENT FOR the Guavian Death Gang, Bala-Tik's patience with Han Solo has been worn out by one too many excuses for failed payments. Bala-Tik brings a group of security soldiers with him to collect what is due from Han.

Armored lining in coat

Gorraslug-leather coat

Percussive cannon

Bala-Tik and the rest of the Guavians carry black market technology, such as experimental percussive cannons.

THE GUAVIAN enforcers are faceless, voiceless cybernetic soldiers, so they rely on Bala-Tik to act as the negotiator in tense confrontations. In the past, Bala-Tik has often been willing to let Solo go, since the Corellian is a good source of money-making leads.

Hunting Solo

Bala-Tik's bosses have ordered him to make an example of Solo. He forges an unlikely alliance with the Kanjiklub gang as they are also owed tens of thousands of credits by Han. After hunting Solo down, Bala-Tik discovers a droid in Solo's possession that the First Order is searching for, and sees an irresistible opportunity to profit.

BARRISS OFFEE

MIRIALAN PADAWAN AND TRAITOR

DATA FILE

AFFILIATION: Jedi
HOMEWORLD: Mirial
SPECIES: Mirialan
HEIGHT: 1.66m (5ft 5in)
APPEARANCES: II
SEE ALSO: Luminara Unduli; Shaak Ti

Mirialan tattoos

PADAWAN BARRISS OFFEE is a thoughtful, daring, and studious Jedi. She is the Padawan learner of Master Luminara Unduli. Barriss is a loyal apprentice who adheres closely to the Jedi Code until the trials of the Clone Wars change her point of view.

Two-handed grip for control

BARRISS OFFEE came to view the Jedi role in the Clone Wars as a betrayal of the Order's ideals. She lashes out against her own kind in a rash and violent manner, orchestrating a bombing of the Jedi Temple and framing a fellow Padawan for the crime. Barriss is discovered and imprisoned.

Belt contains secret compartment

Offee was one of the many Jedi present at the Battle of Geonosis.

Hooded robe

Powerful Team

Offee specialized in tandem fighting and used the Force to keep her actions perfectly in sync with her partner Unduli. The team of Unduli and Offee was more powerful than the sum of its parts.

BATTLE DROID

MECHANICAL DROID SOLDIERS

DATA FILE

AFFILIATION: Separatists
TYPE: B1 battle droid
MANUFACTURER: Baktoid Armor Workshop
HEIGHT: 1.91m (6ft 3in)
APPEARANCES: I, II, III
SEE ALSO: Super battle droid

Simple vocoder

Battle droids are first deployed against the peaceful people of Naboo.

E-5 blaster rifle

Arm extension piston

BATTLE DROIDS are intended to win by strength of numbers rather than by individual ability. The droids are mass-produced and unable to think independently. A computer on board a Trade Federation ship feeds them all their mission commands.

BATTLE DROIDS are the ground troops of the Separatist army: fearless, emotionless, and ready to do their masters' bidding. Battle droids are designed to resemble their Geonosian creators.

Folding knee joint

Limbs resemble humanoid skeletons

STAPs

Battle droid scouts and snipers are swept through the air on armed Single Trooper Aerial Platforms, or STAPs. These repulsorlift vehicles can thread through dense forests that would be inaccessible to larger vehicles.

Pilot droids operate the vast Separatist fleets.

22

BAZE MALBUS

DATA FILE

AFFILIATION: Former Guardian of the Whills
HOMEWORLD: Jedha
SPECIES: Human
HEIGHT: 1.8m (5ft 9in)
APPEARANCES: RO
SEE ALSO: Bodhi Rook; Cassian Andor; Chirrut Îmwe; Jyn Erso; K-2SO

Cooling tank

A BATTLE-HARDENED warrior, Baze operates in Jedha's murky underworld. He takes no interest in politics until the Empire affects him personally. Driven by a thirst for retribution, he joins the Rogue One mission.

Plastoid polymer armor

MWC-35c Staccato Lightning repeating cannon

Weatherproof cloak

Baze and Chirrut Îmwe have conflicting outlooks, but get on well together.

Armored pad for kneeling

BAZE WAS once a Guardian of the Whills, but he abandoned his spiritual side long ago. Now he puts his faith in firepower, embracing modern heavy weapons. He would choose a rocket launcher over a traditional lightbow any day.

Firepower

Baze blasts his way across Scarif with his illegally modified repeating cannon. He puts himself in the firing line to distract the Imperial stormtroopers and shoretroopers while Jyn Erso and Cassian Andor retrieve the Death Star files from the Citadel Tower.

BAZINE NETAL

DEEP COVER SPY

DATA FILE

AFFILIATION: Highest bidder
HOMEWORLD: Chaaktil
SPECIES: Human
HEIGHT: 1.7m (5ft 6in)
APPEARANCES: VII
SEE ALSO: Grummgar;
Kanjiklub gang; Maz Kanata

AN ALLURING and dangerous woman of intrigue lurking in the shadows of Maz Kanata's castle, Bazine Netal is a master of cloak and dagger. She uses her skills of deception to coax secrets from the unwitting and the unwilling.

Custom-styled light-absorbing shroud

Baffleweave patterning

Bazine sits with Grummgar, a big game hunter who frequents Maz Kanata's castle. From this vantage point, Bazine can see all that transpires in the castle.

BAZINE LEARNED

the fundamentals of self-defense living in the dangerous streets of Chaako City, the biggest urban center on Chaaktil. Bazine trained under Delphi Kloda, a grizzled former pirate Kanjiklubber who was the closest thing to a father she ever knew. As a result, Bazine is an expert unarmed combatant.

Vanishing Act

Though Bazine prefers to rely on her own skills rather than technology, she nonetheless keeps sophisticated tools in her arsenal. The complex patterns on her dress are lined with sensor-jamming baffleweave, an electronically impregnated fabric that causes her to disappear from scanner readings.

BB-8

POE DAMERON'S ASTROMECH DROID

DATA FILE

AFFILIATION: Resistance
TYPE: Astromech droid
MANUFACTURER: Industrial Automaton
HEIGHT: 0.67m (2ft 2in)
APPEARANCES: VII, VIII
SEE ALSO: Finn; Poe Dameron; R2-D2; Rey

High-frequency receiver antenna

Primary photoreceptor

Swappable tool bay

AN INTENSELY LOYAL astromech, BB-8 bravely rolls into danger, often on daring missions with Poe Dameron. He is the subject of an intense First Order search when he carries information that could lead to Luke Skywalker.

AS AN ASTROMECH droid, BB-8's small, spherical body is designed to fit into the droid socket of an X-wing starfighter. From that position BB-8 can manage the essential systems of the vessel, make repairs, and plot courses through space.

BB-8 speaks in beeps and whirs, and can project holograms.

Ball Droid

A complex drive system and wireless telemetry keep BB-8 on the move, tumbling his body forward while keeping his head upright. When situations require greater stability, BB-8 can deploy cables from compressed launchers that then anchor the droid in place, or allow him to reel himself into hard-to-reach places.

BERU LARS

LUKE SKYWALKER'S GUARDIAN

DATA FILE

AFFILIATION: None
HOMEWORLD: Tatooine
SPECIES: Human
HEIGHT: 1.65m (5ft 4in)
APPEARANCES: II, III, IV
SEE ALSO: Luke Skywalker;
Owen Lars

Simple hairstyle

BERU LARS' family has been made up of moisture farmers for three generations. At the end of the Clone Wars, Obi-Wan Kenobi asks Beru and her husband, Owen, to raise Luke Skywalker, while he lives nearby to watch over the boy.

Desert tunic

Beru meets Anakin Skywalker when he investigates his mother's kidnapping.

Rough clothing made in Anchorhead

BERU LARS is hard-working and self-reliant. She is well equipped to deal with most of the dangers encountered in the Tatooine desert. However, nothing can prepare Beru for the group of Imperial stormtroopers that come in search of the two renegade droids carrying stolen Death Star plans.

Protector

As Luke becomes a young adult, Beru understands his desire to leave home and join the Imperial Academy. But she also knows the truth about Luke's father, and respects Owen's desire to protect Luke from following in Anakin's footsteps.

Desert boots

BIB FORTUNA

JABBA'S TWI'LEK MAJOR-DOMO

DATA FILE

AFFILIATION: Jabba's court
HOMEWORLD: Ryloth
SPECIES: Twi'lek
HEIGHT: 2m (6ft 6in)
APPEARANCES: I, VI
SEE ALSO: Jabba the Hutt

THE SINISTER BIB FORTUNA
oversees the day-to-day affairs
of Jabba the Hutt's desert palace
and his estate in Mos Eisley.
Before working with Jabba,
Bib Fortuna became rich
as a slave trader of his
own people, the Twi'leks.

Lekku (head-tails;
one of two)

Fortuna hovers near Jabba's
ear, whispering advice.
Secretly, he plots to kill Jabba!

Silver bracelet

Traditional
Ryloth robe

Tricked

Bib Fortuna has been Jabba's
majordomo (head of staff) for
many decades. When two
droids arrive unexpectedly to
bargain for Han Solo's life,
Fortuna unwittingly kickstarts
a chain of events that leads
to the downfall of the
notorious Hutt gangster.

Soft-soled shoes
for silent creeping

BIB FORTUNA is
a powerful and dreaded
individual in Jabba's
entourage. Whether
you are a friend or a
foe, Fortuna will use
underhand means
against you in order
to maintain his control
within the organization.

BISTAN

U-WING DOOR GUNNER

DATA FILE

AFFILIATION: Rebel Alliance
HOMEWORLD: Iakaru
SPECIES: Iakaru
HEIGHT: 1.73m (5ft 7in)
APPEARANCES: RO
SEE ALSO: Pao

Orange eye

BISTAN IS A CORPORAL in the Rebel Alliance Special Forces. He flies with Blue Squadron at the Battle of Scarif, firing his door-mounted ion blaster. Bistan is a ferocious enemy to have, but a fun and sociable squadmate.

Spacesuit sealing ring

THE IAKARU evolved to live in trees, so Bistan has good balance for perching on the ledge of a speeding U-wing. Life in the jungle canopy has also given him keen eyesight, excellent depth perception, and quick reflexes.

On Iakaru, Bistan fought with rocks and spears, but he takes to modern weapons with zeal.

Strength in Numbers

Bistan fled Iakaru when it was overrun by the Empire. Its lush rainforests, full of medicinal plants, are now being plundered by pharmaceutical companies. The best way Bistan can fight for his planet is with the Rebel Alliance.

BOBA FETT

THE BEST BOUNTY HUNTER IN THE GALAXY

DATA FILE

AFFILIATION: Bounty hunter
HOMEWORLD: Kamino
SPECIES: Human clone
HEIGHT: 1.83m (6ft)
APPEARANCES: II, IV, V, VI
SEE ALSO: Darth Vader;
Han Solo; Jabba the Hutt;
Jango Fett

COOL AND CALCULATING, Boba Fett is a legendary bounty hunter. He is paid to track down and, often, kill targeted individuals. Over the years, Fett has developed a code of honor, and only accepts missions that meet this harsh sense of justice.

Multifunction helmet

EE-3 blaster rifle

Reinforced flight suit

Utility belt

On his first mission for Vader, Boba unwittingly reveals that Vader's son is alive by discovering that a Skywalker destroyed the Death Star.

BOBA FETT'S talent and skill, combined with an arsenal of exotic weapons, has brought in many "impossible" bounties. He is notorious for completely disintegrating those whom he has been hired to track down.

Like Father, Like Son

Boba Fett is an exact genetic clone of Jango Fett, who brings Boba up as a son. Boba witnesses Jango's death at the Battle of Geonosis and swears revenge against the Jedi who killed him. In time, he inherits Jango Fett's Mandalorian battle armor and his ship, *Slave I*.

Working for Darth Vader, Fett captures Han Solo and loads his carbon-frozen body into *Slave I*.

BOBBAJO

CRITTERMONGER AND STORYTELLER

DATA FILE

AFFILIATION: None
HOMEWORLD: Jakku
SPECIES: Nu-Cosian
HEIGHT: 1.14m (3ft 7in)
APPEARANCES: VII
SEE ALSO: Rey; Teedo;
Unkar Plutt

SHUFFLING HIS rare animal merchandise to various marketplaces and trading posts is Bobbajo, known to many simply as the Crittermonger. He is also known as the Storyteller, for his habit of spinning long and unlikely yarns.

Sneep

Head wrapping

Long, flexible neck

THE CREAKY-JOINTED Nu-Cosian
has an unflappable, kind personality that has a calming effect on the jittery creatures he keeps in his cages. It also lends a magical quality to his storytelling, as his gentle nature attracts many listeners.

Old Wanderer
Bobbajo has been a fixture on Jakku and nearby worlds for decades. To ensure he always has exotic merchandise, he braves the most treacherous terrain, including the crumbling cliffs of Carbon Ridge. He trudges through the shifting landscape as if following his own peculiar rhythm, ignoring the many dangers that surround him.

BODHI ROOK

IMPERIAL DEFECTOR

DATA FILE

AFFILIATION: Empire, Rebel Alliance, Rogue One
HOMEWORLD: Jedha
SPECIES: Human
HEIGHT: 1.75m (5ft 7in)
APPEARANCES: RO
SEE ALSO: Galen Erso; Jyn Erso; Saw Gerrera

Flight goggles

Weatherproof poncho for Eadu's wet climate

Imperial flight suit

BODHI ROOK was an ordinary pilot, who flew cargo for the Empire. One day he is given a message that could change the course of the galaxy. It turns him into an Imperial deserter, a wanted man—and a rebel hero.

WHEN BODHI wasn't ferrying kyber crystals from Jedha to the Imperial research facility on Eadu, he gambled on odupiendo races. Watching these super-fast running birds honed his piloting skills, giving him an eye for speed and tactics.

Bodhi gets Rogue One clearance to pass through the secure shield gate at Scarif—and even gives the ship its name.

Brave Messenger

Delivering Galen Erso's message to the rebels is not easy. Finding Saw Gerrera without being killed is hard enough for Bodhi, but convincing him of the truth is impossible. Deeply suspicious, Gerrera interrogates Bodhi with help from a terrifying Mairan, Bor Gullet, and then locks him up. Bodhi finds he is more courageous than he thought.

BOSS NASS

GUNGAN LEADER

DATA FILE

AFFILIATION: Gungan Rep Council, Gungan Grand Army
HOMEWORLD: Naboo
SPECIES: Gungan
HEIGHT: 2.06m (6ft 8in)
APPEARANCES: I, III
SEE ALSO: Jar Jar Binks; Padmé Amidala

Crown of rulership

Epaulets of military authority

Four-fingered hand

The Gungan High Council has the power to summon the Gungan Grand Army.

BOSS NASS

sits on the Gungan High Council. He is a fair but stubborn ruler. He particularly resents the Naboo's belief that the Gungans are primitive simply because Gungans prefer to use traditional crafts and technologies.

Long coat with golden clasp

BOSS NASS is the stern, old-fashioned ruler of Otoh Gunga, the largest of the Gungan underwater cities on Naboo. He speaks Galactic Basic (the most widely used language in the galaxy) with a strong accent.

For Jar Jar's help during the Naboo blockade, Nass reverses his banishment from Otoh Gunga.

Teamwork

When his planet is faced with invasion, Boss Nass puts aside his prejudice against the Naboo. He receives Queen Amidala when she humbly asks him for help. Boss Nass realizes that his people must work together with the Naboo or die, and a new friendship is forged between the two cultures.

BOSSK

TRANDOSHAN BOUNTY HUNTER

Eyes can see in infrared range

DATA FILE

AFFILIATION: Bounty hunter
HOMEWORLD: Trandosha
SPECIES: Trandoshan
HEIGHT: 1.9m (6ft 2in)
APPEARANCES: V, VI
SEE ALSO: Aurra Sing;
Boba Fett; Darth Vader

THE TOUGH AND RESILIENT Bossk is a reptilian Trandoshan bounty hunter. He used to track runaway slaves. Now he claims bounties for the Empire, and is incredibly successful at capturing his prey.

Sling for grenade launcher

Flak vest

Relby v-10 micro grenade launcher

BOSSK began his career doing a form of bounty hunting that few other species would risk: hunting Wookiees. Later, he hunts other species. During the Clone Wars, Bossk teams up with Aurra Sing, young Boba Fett, and a Klatooinian bounty hunter named Castas.

Lost fingers, skin, and even limbs can regrow until adulthood

Bossk and other bounty hunters frequently visit Jabba the Hutt, seeking their next job.

Tough Trandoshan

Fond of skinning his captives when possible, Bossk is as vile and mean as bounty hunters get. He is one of the six bounty hunters Darth Vader enlists to track down and capture the *Millennium Falcon*.

BOUSHH

PRINCESS LEIA IN DISGUISE

DATA FILE

AFFILIATION: Bounty hunter
HOMEWORLD: Uba IV
SPECIES: Ubese
HEIGHT: 1.5m (4ft 9in)
APPEARANCES: VI
SEE ALSO: Chewbacca;
Jabba the Hutt;
Princess Leia

Speech scrambler

Glove spikes

Projectile detonator

Ammo pouch

Leia, in disguise as Boushh, prepares to release Han Solo from frozen captivity.

BOUSHH battles Leia on Ord Mantell, where Leia travels seeking help to free Han Solo from carbonite. Maz Kanata helps Leia defeat Boushh so Leia can use his armor and helmet as a disguise to fool Jabba the Hutt.

THE GALAXY contains many bizarre creatures acting as bounty hunters (or claiming to be). Princess Leia adopts a convincing identity as an Ubese tracker, Boushh, to gain entry to Jabba's palace. Only Jabba suspects her identity is false.

Shata leather pants

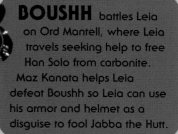

Jabba's suspicions prove correct as he catches Leia unmasked with Han.

Boushh's Bounty

At Jabba's palace, Chewbacca pretends to be Boushh's captive, and Boushh demands a high price for the captured Wookiee. When Jabba disagrees over the amount of credits, Boushh pulls out a thermal detonator.

Traditional Ubese boots

C-3PO

GOLDEN PROTOCOL DROID

DATA FILE

AFFILIATION: Republic/ Rebel Alliance/Resistance
TYPE: Protocol droid
MANUFACTURER: Cybot Galactica
HEIGHT: 1.67m (5ft 5in)
APPEARANCES: I, II, III, RO, IV, V, VI, VII, VIII
SEE ALSO: Anakin Skywalker; Luke Skywalker; R2-D2

Vocabulator

C-3PO IS PROGRAMMED to assist in matters of etiquette and translation. Thrown into a world of adventure, he is often overwhelmed by the action around him. But he forms a capable team when partnered with the resourceful R2-D2.

Bronzium finish polished to a dazzling shine

Primary power coupling outlet

Anakin Skywalker built the working skeleton of C-3PO from scrap parts.

Reinforced knee joint

C-3PO first works for Anakin Skywalker and his mother, Shmi. Anakin then gives C-3PO to Senator Padmé Amidala as a wedding gift. After Padmé's death, C-3PO is assigned to Bail Organa, until Darth Vader captures the *Tantive IV*. C-3PO escapes to Tatooine and is sold to Luke Skywalker.

Golden God

Despite his fear of excitement, C-3PO has led an adventurous life, often losing limbs or bits of circuitry along the way (though he is easily repaired). On Endor, a tribe of Ewoks worships C-3PO as a "golden god," which leads the Ewoks to support the rebels and play a decisive role in defeating the Empire.

C'AI THRENALI

HOTSHOT PILOT

DATA FILE

AFFILIATION: Resistance
HOMEWORLD: Abednedo
SPECIES: Abednedo
HEIGHT: Unknown
APPEARANCES: VII, VIII
SEE ALSO: Lieutenant Connix;
Poe Dameron

Dangling mouth
tentacles

C'AI THRENALI is Poe Dameron's wingman in the Resistance Starfighter Corps. As comfortable flying an X-wing starfighter as much as a regular airspeeder, he can turn his hand to any controls.

C'ai Threnali is an Abednedo like Ello Asty, one of the pilots who helped to destroy Starkiller base.

MANY ABEDNEDO

have integrated into life across the galaxy. They mix well with other species thanks to their sociability, intelligence, and curiosity. In his orange flight suit, C'ai blends in with the rest of the rebel pilots, except for his specially shaped helmet.

Lucky Survivor

C'ai is loyal to Poe Dameron and sides with him in his mutiny against Vice Admiral Holdo. However, in the end, C'ai survives the D'Qar evacuation thanks to Holdo's plan and her self-sacrifice. He is also one of the few rebels who live to tell the tale of the Battle of Crait.

Signal flares

Feet have
three toes

CANTO BIGHT POLICE

CORRUPT OFFICERS OF THE LAW

DATA FILE

AFFILIATION: Canto Bight Police Department
SPECIES: Human
STANDARD EQUIPMENT: Relby K-25 blaster; electro-shock stun prod
APPEARANCES: VIII
SEE ALSO: Finn; Rose Tico

Mirror-image lettering

THE CANTO BIGHT Police Department maintains order in the casino-city on Cantonica. However, it concerns itself more with appearances than with its poorer citizens. Its priority is the rich visitors: if they feel safe and valued, then they will keep spending.

Flexible betaplast neck guard

Betaplast armored collar

POLICE uniforms are designed to give guests reassurance, while also being equipped for swift, discrete action against anyone who disturbs the peace. Officers do not want an ugly scene to damage the city's reputation.

The police headquarters and surveillance building sits on a hill near Canto Bight, overlooking the city.

INIQUITY

Penalties are high for anyone who disrupts Canto Bight's lavishly maintained public areas—like Rose and Finn who park their starfighter on a beach. However, more serious crime can be overlooked—if you're rich enough to bribe the police.

Electro-shock stun prod

CAPTAIN ANTILLES

CAPTAIN OF THE *TANTIVE IV*

DATA FILE

AFFILIATION: Republic/
Rebel Alliance
HOMEWORLD: Alderaan
SPECIES: Human
HEIGHT: 1.88m (6ft 2in)
APPEARANCES: III, IV, RO
SEE ALSO: Bail Organa;
Princess Leia

CAPTAIN RAYMUS ANTILLES is commander of Bail Organa's fleet of diplomatic cruisers. Under the Empire, Antilles becomes a rebel and serves as captain of the *Tantive IV* under Organa's adopted daughter, Leia Organa.

Cape of
Alderaanian
nobility

Wrist guard

CAPTAIN ANTILLES is a highly capable pilot. He has taken part in many daring missions for the rebels, and has had notable success breaking through Imperial blockades.

Target blaster

The Alderaan royal family owns the diplomatic cruiser *Tantive IV*.

Flight boots

Stranglehold

In the battle over Tatooine, Darth Vader boards the *Tantive IV* and demands that Antilles surrenders the stolen Death Star plans. When he refuses, Vader destroys him.

CRIMSON CORSAIR

CAPTAIN ITHANO

DATA FILE

AFFILIATION: None
HOMEWORLD: Unknown
SPECIES: Delphidian
HEIGHT: 1.93m (6ft 3in)
APPEARANCES: VII
SEE ALSO: Finn; Maz Kanata

THE ERA OF LAWLESSNESS that follows the Galactic Civil War leads to the rise of the colorful pirate, Sidon Ithano. Ithano uses many flashy aliases, and tales of his exploits continue to grow.

Captured Kanjiklub rifle

Pirate Crew

Ithano pilots the *Meson Martinet*, and his pirate crew (which includes his one-legged First Mate Quiggold) runs a smooth ship. Finn very nearly joins Ithano's crew at Maz's castle, when he tries to find a new life after deserting from the First Order.

Armorweave-lined cape

Ithano's polished Kaleesh war helmet conceals his Delphidian features.

ITHANO IS

extremely vain, and relishes stories of his deeds as the "Blood Buccaneer," the "Crimson Corsair," or the "Red Raider." He lets these stories do the hard work for him, as many targeted vessels surrender without putting up a fight.

CAPTAIN NEEDA

COMMANDER OF THE *AVENGER*

DATA FILE

AFFILIATION: Empire
HOMEWORLD: Coruscant
SPECIES: Human
HEIGHT: 1.75m (5ft 7in)
APPEARANCES: V
SEE ALSO: Admiral Ozzel;
Darth Vader

CAPTAIN NEEDA IS COMMANDER
of the Imperial Star Destroyer *Avenger*,
which takes part in the search for the
rebels' hidden bases. Needa follows
the *Falcon* into an asteroid field
and back out, but then loses
the ship completely.

Standard-issue
officer's gloves

Imperial officer's tunic

Belt buckle with
data storage

LORTH NEEDA is a
dependable and ruthless officer
who served the Galactic Republic
in the Clone Wars during the
Battle of Coruscant, when General
Grievous "kidnapped" Chancellor
Palpatine. Now an Imperial
officer, Needa fails to live up
to Vader's exacting standards.

Needa fails to see that the *Millennium
Falcon* "disappeared" by clinging to
the side of his Star Destroyer.

No Mercy

When Needa loses sight of the *Falcon*,
he apologizes to Vader, accepting full
responsibility. Vader accepts Needa's
apology—then Force-chokes him.

CAPTAIN PANAKA

NABOO HEAD OF SECURITY

DATA FILE

AFFILIATION: Royal Naboo Security Forces
HOMEWORLD: Naboo
SPECIES: Human
HEIGHT: 1.83m (6ft)
APPEARANCES: I
SEE ALSO: Padmé Amidala

AS HEAD OF SECURITY for Queen Amidala on Naboo, Captain Quarsh Panaka oversees every branch of the volunteer Royal Naboo Security Forces. During the invasion of Naboo, Panaka sees the dangerous state of affairs in the galaxy and argues for stronger security.

Leather jerkin

Utility belt

CAPTAIN PANAKA
gained combat experience in a Republic Special Task Force, fighting against space pilots in the sector containing the Naboo system.

High officer headgear

Stripes on coat indicate rank

After Queen Amidala's abdication, Panaka serves Queen Jamillia.

Royal Responsibility

Panaka is responsible for Queen Amidala's safety, accompanying her during the escape from Naboo. When the queen returns to Naboo to reclaim her throne, Panaka is by her side, offering cover fire during the infiltration of the palace.

CAPTAIN PHASMA

STORMTROOPER COMMANDER

CLAD IN DISTINCTIVE metallic armor, Captain Phasma commands the First Order's legions of stormtroopers. She sees it as her duty to ensure only the best soldiers serve the First Order.

Chromium-plated
F-11D blaster rifle

Crush gauntlets

Armorweave cape

When FN-2187, a stormtrooper under her command, abandons his duties and defects to the Resistance, Phasma takes it as a personal failing.

DESPITE HER RANK, Phasma prefers being in the thick of combat operations, witnessing battle firsthand and fighting alongside her troops. Her armor is coated in salvaged Naboo chromium that offers protection and emphasizes her authority.

Forged in Battle

Phasma believes that true soldiers are only made in combat. Though she recognizes the value of the complex simulations used in stormtrooper training, she thinks that success in simulations is no real guarantee of a soldier's bravery.

CAPTAIN TYPHO

SENATOR AMIDALA'S HEAD OF SECURITY

DATA FILE

AFFILIATION: Royal Naboo Security Forces
HOMEWORLD: Naboo
SPECIES: Human
HEIGHT: 1.85m (6ft 1in)
APPEARANCES: II, III
SEE ALSO: Captain Panaka; Padmé Amidala

Security uniform

Eye lost during Battle of Naboo

CAPTAIN TYPHO is well respected for his loyalty. His uncle, Captain Panaka, was head of security for Padmé Amidala when she was Queen of Naboo. Now Typho oversees security for Padmé in her role as Senator for Naboo.

Synthetic leather gauntlets

Naboo blaster

AT THE TIME of the Battle of Naboo, Typho was a Junior Palace Guard. Despite his young age, Typho played a brave part in the conflict, losing his eye in the line of duty. Captain Typho is given his Senatorial post because of his loyalty and his ties to Panaka.

Captain Typho is by Amidala's side on many missions throughout the Clone Wars.

A Dangerous World

Captain Typho accompanies Senator Amidala to Coruscant, where an assassination attempt kills seven in his command, including Padmé's handmaiden Cordé (disguised as Padmé). Typho soon realizes that even his strict security measures might not be enough in the new, dangerous world of the Clone Wars.

43

CASSIAN ANDOR

REBEL INTELLIGENCE AGENT

DATA FILE

AFFILIATION: Rebel Alliance, Rogue One
HOMEWORLD: Fest
SPECIES: Human
HEIGHT: 1.78m (5ft 9in)
APPEARANCES: RO
SEE ALSO: Jyn Erso; K-2SO

CAPTAIN CASSIAN ANDOR lives and breathes the Rebellion. His role in military intelligence often puts him on the front line, gathering snippets of information that could be used against the Empire. He goes by many names and blends into a crowd.

Captain's pips

Corellian-style field jacket

BlasTech A280-CFE weapon

CASSIAN JERON Andor

has been caught up in violence since the Clone Wars came to his home planet, Fest, when he was six years old. His traumatic experiences make him all the more determined to disrupt the Empire. He fights it with whatever minor acts of rebellion he can: sabotage, attacks, or assassinations.

Cassian is able to call on a network of informants across the galaxy for intelligence vital to the Rebel cause.

Going Rogue

For an intelligence officer, there is no greater prize than the files of the Death Star. Stealing them from under the Empire's nose means going on a suicide mission, against orders. But the data gets through: mission complete.

CHANCELLOR VALORUM

DATA FILE

AFFILIATION: Republic
HOMEWORLD: Coruscant
SPECIES: Human
HEIGHT: 1.7m (5ft 6in)
APPEARANCES: I
SEE ALSO: Mas Amedda;
Padmé Amidala; Palpatine

BEFORE PALPATINE becomes Supreme Chancellor, Finis Valorum holds the highest position in the Galactic Senate. He rules the Republic when Trade Federation warships blockade the peaceful planet of Naboo. Padmé Amidala blames Valorum personally.

Ornate overcloak

Blue band symbolic of Supreme Chancellor

When Valorum resigns, Senator Palpatine steps in, promising strength and effectiveness.

Veda cloth robe

VALORUM comes from a family of politicians. All his life, he has been preparing for the office of Supreme Chancellor. This is a man who enjoys the privileges of a head of state. However, this attitude does not endear him to ordinary voters.

Weak Leader

While Naboo suffers, the Senate debates its options, but does not act. The Speaker, Mas Amedda (secretly working for Palpatine), knows that this indecision will make Valorum look weak and ineffective.

CHEWBACCA

WOOKIEE WARRIOR, PILOT, AND HERO

DATA FILE

AFFILIATION: Rebel Alliance/Resistance
HOMEWORLD: Kashyyyk
SPECIES: Wookiee
HEIGHT: 2.28m (7ft 5in)
APPEARANCES: III, S, IV, V, VI, VII, VIII
SEE ALSO: Han Solo; Tarfful

Bowcaster

Water-shedding hair

Tool pouch

CHEWBACCA is a Wookiee mechanic and pilot. During the Clone Wars, he fights to defend his planet. Under the Empire, he is first mate, mechanic, and loyal friend to Han Solo aboard the *Millennium Falcon*.

CHEWIE SERVES

as Han Solo's fiercely loyal copilot and trusty fellow adventurer. He enjoys the thrilling action that Solo gets them into, but sometimes tries to act as a check on his partner's willfulness.

Unlikely Friendship

Chewbacca first meets Han Solo in an Imperial prison pit on Mimban, and they get off to a violent start. Han is supposed to be Chewie's dinner, but he manages to escape and takes the Wookiee along for the ride.

Thirty years after the Rebellion, Han and Chewie are still side by side.

CHIEF CHIRPA

WISE CHIEF CHIRPA has led the Bright Tree tribe on the forest moon of Endor for 42 seasons. When his Ewok tribe captures a Rebel Alliance strike force, Chirpa is only stopped from sacrificing them by C-3PO, whom the superstitious Ewoks believe is a "golden god."

DATA FILE

AFFILIATION: Bright Tree Village

HOMEWORLD: Forest moon of Endor

SPECIES: Ewok

HEIGHT: 1m (3ft 3in)

APPEARANCES: VI

SEE ALSO: Logray; Teebo

Hood

Acute sense of smell

Reptilian staff

Chief's medallion

CHIEF Chirpa leads his village with understanding, though he has become a bit forgetful in his old age. His authority commits the Ewoks to their dangerous fight against the Empire.

Hunting knife

The Bright Tree tribe lives in a village high up in the treetops.

New Recruits

After listening to C-3PO's account of the resistance to the Empire, Chirpa commits the Ewoks to the struggle. In the Battle of Endor, the Ewok warriors use all their cunning and fierceness to defeat the superior forces of the Imperial Army.

CHIRRUT ÎMWE

GUARDIAN OF THE WHILLS

DATA FILE

AFFILIATION: Guardian of the Whills
HOMEWORLD: Jedha
SPECIES: Human
HEIGHT: 1.73m (5ft 7in)
APPEARANCES: RO
SEE ALSO: Baze Malbus; Bodhi Rook; Cassian Andor; Jyn Erso; K-2SO

CHIRRUT ÎMWE may not be able to see with his eyes, but that does not stop him from being a formidable warrior. With intense training and focus, he has turned his body into a skilled fighting machine. Îmwe is intensely spiritual and believes deeply in the Force.

Gauntlet for steadying lightbow shots

Lightbow slung over shoulder

Staff made of uneti wood

AS GUARDIAN of the Whills, Îmwe belongs to an ancient order of warrior monks. Its main role is to protect the Temple of the Kyber in the Holy City of Jedha. This sacred job becomes obsolete when the whole city is destroyed by a single test shot from the Death Star.

Ancient kasaya robes

Îmwe knocks down stormtroopers with elegant but deadly twirls of his uneti-wood staff.

Warrior Monk

The battlefield on Scarif is daunting even if you have full sight. Muttering mantras gives Îmwe strength to face the enemy against terrible odds. He is a master of the martial art zama-shiwo, so he can achieve a peaceful mental and physical state. He gains control over his body, even his heart rate and oxygen intake.

CLIEGG LARS

SHMI SKYWALKER'S HUSBAND

WHEN TATOOINIAN moisture farmer Cliegg Lars goes looking for a farmhand in Mos Espa, he instead meets a slave and falls in love. The slave is Shmi Skywalker, Anakin Skywalker's mother. In order to marry Shmi, Cliegg buys her freedom from Watto, the flying junk dealer who owns her.

Gear harness

Weather-worn work clothes

Cliegg loses a leg in his attempt to rescue Shmi from Tusken Raiders.

CLIEGG'S father was a Tatooinian farmer, but young Cliegg wanted to experience life on a bustling Core World. Here, he fell in love with and married Aika. But when Aika died, Cliegg returned to Tatooine to run the family farm.

Heartbroken

Cliegg loses Shmi when Tusken Raiders kidnap and kill her. After her death, Cliegg remains determined to live the life he has worked so hard to create. Sadly, he dies shortly afterward from a broken heart.

CLONE PILOT

SPECIALIST CLONE AIRMEN

DATA FILE

AFFILIATION:
Republic/Empire
SPECIES: Human clone
STANDARD EQUIPMENT:
DC-15a blaster; thermal
detonators; ammunition
APPEARANCES: II, III
SEE ALSO: Clone trooper

Anti-glare
blast visor

Rebreather
unit

Air-supply hose

FROM THE START of the Clone Wars, clones were trained to fly LAAT gunships. As the war progresses, a new breed are trained to fly the hyperspace-capable ARC-170 and V-wing starfighters.

A pilot and copilot/forward gunner fly an ARC-170 fighter at the Battle of Coruscant.

Flight data
records pouch

IN THE BATTLE OF

Coruscant, most clone pilots wear Phase II pilot armor, with helmets fitted with anti-glare blast visors. V-wing pilots, however, wear fully enclosed helmets since these ships carry no on-board life-support systems.

Gunship Pilots

At the start of the Clone Wars, in the Battle of Geonosis, clone pilots fly LAAT/i and LAAT/c gunships. They wear Phase I battle armor, distinguished by yellow markings and specialized full-face helmets.

CLONE TROOPER (PHASE I)

FIRST GENERATION CLONE TROOPERS

DATA FILE

AFFILIATION: Republic
HOMEWORLD: Kamino
SPECIES: Human clone
HEIGHT: 1.83m (6ft)
APPEARANCES: II
SEE ALSO: Clone trooper (Phase II); clone pilot; Jango Fett

Clone troopers are deployed from Republic assault ships, which also carry gunships.

DC-15 blaster

Breath filter

Utility belt

Thigh plate

THE FIRST CLONE troopers are designated Phase I because of their style of armor. Born and raised in Kaminoan cloning factories, they are trained for no other purpose than to fight, and feel virtually invincible.

PHASE I armor is loosely based on Jango Fett's Mandalorian shock trooper armor. It consists of 20 armor plates and is often referred to as the "body bucket" because it is heavy and uncomfortable.

High-traction soles

First Strike

When the Separatist droid army makes its first all-out strike on Geonosis, the Senate has no choice but to send in an army of clone soldiers that it has neither amassed nor trained. Under the skillful command of the Jedi, the clones force a droid retreat.

CLONE TROOPER (PHASE II)

SECOND GENERATION CLONE TROOPERS

DATA FILE

AFFILIATION: Republic/Empire
HOMEWORLD: Kamino
SPECIES: Human clone
HEIGHT: 1.83m (6ft)
APPEARANCES: III
SEE ALSO: Clone trooper
(Phase I)

Clone troopers form the galaxy's best military force.

Battle-damaged chest plastron

Spare blaster magazine

Standard DC-15 blaster has a folding stock

BY THE TIME of the Battle of Coruscant, clone troopers, with enhanced Phase II armor, are battle-dented and mud-smeared. Aging at twice the rate of normally birthed humans, only two-thirds of the original army of clone troopers are alive.

Knee plate

PHASE II armor is stronger, lighter, and more adaptable than Phase I armor, and has many specialist variations.

Superior Troopers
Clone troopers are equipped with far more advanced armor and air support than the Separatists, allowing them to easily cut through the battle droid ranks.

COLEMAN TREBOR

VURK JEDI MASTER

DATA FILE

AFFILIATION: Jedi
HOMEWORLD: Sembla
SPECIES: Vurk
HEIGHT: 2.13m (7ft)
APPEARANCES: II
SEE ALSO: Count Dooku;
Yarael Poof

Bony head
crest grows
throughout
life

Thick
reptilian skin

Coleman Trebor joined the Jedi
High Council after the death of Jedi
Master Yarael Poof.

Food and
energy capsules

Jedi cloak

JEDI MASTER Coleman
Trebor is revered as
a skillful mediator,
bringing difficult disputes
to a harmonious end.
His skill with a lightsaber
is also impressive,
and he joins Windu's
taskforce to Geonosis.

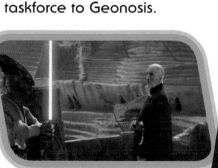

Facing Dooku

On Geonosis, Coleman Trebor
seizes his opportunity and steps
up to Count Dooku, taking the
Separatist leader by surprise. But
bounty hunter Jango Fett quickly
fires his blaster at the noble
Jedi, who falls to his death.

COLEMAN TREBOR

is a Vurk from the oceanic world
of Sembla. His species is thought
to be primitive, but they are in
fact highly empathetic and
serene. Trebor's Force potential
was spotted early on, and he
joined the Jedi Order, the only
Vurk known to have done so.

COMMANDER BLY

AAYLA SECURA'S CLONE COMMANDER

DATA FILE

AFFILIATION:
Republic/Empire
HOMEWORLD: Kamino
SPECIES: Human clone
HEIGHT: 1.83m (6ft)
APPEARANCES: III
SEE ALSO: Aayla Secura;
Clone trooper (Phase II)

Helmet contains oxygen supply

After Order 66 turns him against the Republic, Bly serves the Empire.

Plastoid armor pitted from shrapnel strikes

COMMANDER BLY
is a clone of Jango Fett. He was part of the first wave of clone commanders trained by the Advanced Recon Commando (ARC) troopers. Bly's focus is entirely on the success of each mission.

Quick-release holster for DC-17 repeater hand blaster

Cold Commander

Clone Commander Bly and Jedi General Aayla Secura are hunting down Separatist leader Shu Mai on the exotic world of Felucia when Bly receives Palpatine's Order 66. Without a moment's hesitation, the clone soldier guns down the Jedi Knight he had served with on so many missions.

CLONE COMMANDER

CC-5052, or Bly, has worked closely with Jedi General Aayla Secura, and respects her dedication to completing the mission.

COMMANDER CODY

OBI-WAN KENOBI'S CLONE COMMANDER

DATA FILE

AFFILIATION: Republic/Empire
HOMEWORLD: Kamino
SPECIES: Human clone
HEIGHT: 1.83m (6ft)
APPEARANCES: III
SEE ALSO: Clone trooper (Phase II); Obi-Wan Kenobi

Breath filter

This variant of Phase II armor features one antenna

Cody's last loyal action is to return Kenobi's lost lightsaber to the Jedi.

DC-15 blaster rifle yields 300 shots on maximum power

CLONE UNIT 2224, known as Commander Cody, is often assigned to Jedi General Obi-Wan Kenobi. He is one of the original clones from Kamino. His extra training developed leadership ability.

Color denotes legion affiliation

CLONE COMMANDERS

like Cody use names in addition to numerical designations. The Jedi and progressive-thinking Republic officials initiated this practice in order to foster a growing fellowship. This is why CC-2224 came to be called Cody.

High-traction boots

Sidious in Charge

Cody fights loyally and bravely alongside General Kenobi on many missions in the Clone Wars, including on Lola Sayu and Utapau. They have established an easy-going camaraderie. Nevertheless, when Cody receives Palpatine's Order 66 to destroy the Jedi, he does so without giving his betrayal a second thought.

COMMANDER GREE

SENIOR CLONE COMMANDER ON KASHYYYK

Polarized
T-visor

Camouflage
markings

Weapons and
ammunition belt

CLONE UNIT 1004
chose the name Gree to
express his interest in the
wide and varied alien
cultures found throughout
the galaxy. The Gree is a
little-known alien species.

Reinforced
tactical boots

Armor
plates are
often replaced

Ultimately loyal only to Palpatine,
Gree attempts to kill Yoda. But
Yoda strikes down the clone.

CLONE COMMANDER GREE
commands the 41st Elite Corps
in the Clone Wars. Led by Jedi
General Luminara Unduli, the 41st
specializes in long-term missions
on alien worlds. Gree uses his
knowledge of the customs of
alien species to help build
alliances with local populations.

Wookiee Defenders

Gree serves under Jedi Master Yoda at
the Battle of Kashyyyk. Gree's camouflage
armor provides cover in the green jungles
of the Wookiee planet. His battle-hardened
clone troopers are also equipped
for jungle warfare.

COMMANDER NEYO

STASS ALLIE'S CLONE COMMANDER

Enhanced
breath filter

CLONE COMMANDER NEYO
is assigned to the 91st
Reconnaissance Corps, which
often utilizes BARC speeders.
Neyo fights many battles
in the Outer Rim sieges
during the Clone Wars.

ARC
command sash

Built-in comlink

Equipment
pouch

Regiment markings

Neyo serves with Jedi Stass
Allie in the siege of the
Separatist planet Saleucami.

NEYO, OR UNIT 8826, is
one of the first 100 graduates from
the experimental clone commander
training program on Kamino. Bred
solely for fighting, Neyo developed
a disturbingly cold personality.

Clone Betrayal
After the Republic captures Saleucami,
Neyo stays on to destroy the last
pockets of resistance. During a speeder
patrol with Stass Allie, Neyo receives
Order 66 and turns his laser
cannons on the Jedi General.

COUNT DOOKU

SEPARATIST LEADER AND SITH LORD

DATA FILE

AFFILIATION: Sith, Separatists
HOMEWORLD: Serenno
SPECIES: Human
HEIGHT: 1.93m (6ft 3in)
APPEARANCES: II, III
SEE ALSO: Anakin Skywalker; Palpatine

Cape is emblem of Count of Serenno

Curved lightsaber hilt

Caught between Anakin's blades, Dooku is unprepared for Sidious's treachery.

COUNT DOOKU was once a Jedi Master. But his independent spirit led him away from the Order and he became a Sith apprentice, named Darth Tyranus. As Dooku, he leads the Separatist movement, which seeks independence from the Republic.

COUNT DOOKU

is a member of the nobility on his homeworld of Serenno, and one of the richest men in the galaxy. He uses his wealth and power to convince many star systems to join his Separatist movement.

Boots of rare rancor leather

During the first battle of Geonosis, Dooku fights Yoda—his former master.

Sith Skills

Count Dooku is a formidable opponent. In combat, his style is characterized by graceful moves and cunning prowess. He can also project deadly streams of Sith Force lightning from his fingertips.

DARTH VADER

DARK LORD OF THE SITH

DATA FILE

AFFILIATION: Sith, Empire
HOMEWORLD: Tatooine
SPECIES: Human
HEIGHT: (in armor)
2.02m (6ft 6in)
APPEARANCES: III, RO,
IV, V, VI
SEE ALSO: Anakin
Skywalker; Luke Skywalker;
Palpatine

Vader fights Obi-Wan in the battle that will result in his encasement in a life-support suit.

THE GRIM, forbidding figure of Darth Vader is Emperor Palpatine's Sith apprentice and a much-feared military commander. Vader's knowledge of the dark side of the Force makes him unnerving and dangerous.

Primary control panel

AFTER VADER'S near-fatal duel with Obi-Wan, Palpatine has his apprentice encased in black armor. Vader is unable to survive without the constant life support provided by his black suit.

Sinister outer cloak

Father and Son

When Vader learns that Luke Skywalker is his son, he harbors a desire to turn Luke to the dark side and rule the galaxy with him. Yet Luke refuses to lose sight of Vader's humanity under the armor.

Vader misses retrieving the stolen Death Star plans from the rebels by mere moments.

DEATH STAR GUNNER

IMPERIAL WEAPONS OPERATORS

DATA FILE

AFFILIATION: Empire
SPECIES: Human
HEIGHT: 1.8m (5ft 9in)
APPEARANCES: RO, IV, VI
SEE ALSO: AT-AT pilot;
AT-ST pilot; Stormtrooper

Energy-shielded fabric

Black durasteel gloves

Gunners on platforms monitor the titanic energy levels of the Death Star's superlaser.

DEATH STAR GUNNERS control the terrible weapons of the Empire's capital ships, military bases, and Death Star battlestations. Their elite skills with weapons are used to handle powerful turbolasers and ion cannons.

THE IMPERIAL Navy equips Death Star gunners with specialized helmets with slit-eye like visors, designed to protect their eyes from the bright flashes of light from turbolaser and superlaser fire. Many gunners find that the helmets restrict all-round vision.

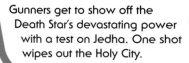

Gunners get to show off the Death Star's devastating power with a test on Jedha. One shot wipes out the Holy City.

Turbolaser Gunners

The Empire's capital ships and its Death Star are bristling with turbolasers. A team of gunners man these heavy guns, which rotate on turrets. The gunners monitor crucial recharge timings and heat levels, while locking onto targets. A single blast can obliterate an enemy starfighter.

DEATH TROOPER

ELITE STORMTROOPERS

DATA FILE

AFFILIATION: Empire
SPECIES: Human (augmented)
STANDARD EQUIPMENT:
E-11D blaster rifle; DLT-19D heavy blaster rifle; SE-14r light repeating blaster; C-25 fragmentation grenade
APPEARANCES: RO
SEE ALSO: Orson Krennic; Stormtrooper

E-11D blaster rifle

Krennic sends a cadre of his death troopers to defend Scarif against the rebel incursion.

Reflec polymer coating on armor warps electromagnet signals

C-25 fragmentation grenade

STORMTROOPERS who show particular potential can become the elite: black-armored death troopers. They are tasked with protecting the most senior Imperial officers, like those of the Tarkin Initiative.

Loyal Followers

As Director Orson Krennic's personal security force, death troopers accompany him everywhere. On the backwater planet of Lah'mu, they provide the force for the "collection" of the scientist Galen Erso.

AT A SPECIALIST

camp on Scarif, death troopers are trained to be tougher, faster, and more resilient than regular stormtroopers. They even undergo physical augmentation to boost their abilities.

Flexible leather boots

DEPA BILLABA

DATA FILE

AFFILIATION: Jedi
HOMEWORLD: Chalacta
SPECIES: Human
HEIGHT: 1.68m (5ft 5in)
APPEARANCES: I, II
SEE ALSO: Mace Windu;
Qui-Gon Jinn; Yoda

Chalactan marks
of illumination

Billaba offers an ordered
perspective to the wide-ranging
minds of her fellow Jedi.

Jedi robes cover
practical fighting tunic

Lightsaber
worn on utility
belt under robes

JEDI MASTER Depa
Billaba serves on the
Jedi High Council
where she is known
to be a wise and
spiritual voice. She
serves as a Jedi
General during
the Clone Wars.

BILLABA'S FORCES

suffered a devastating loss
against General Grievous at
Haruun Kal. The battle's physical
and psychological toll caused
some among the Jedi to wonder
if she would ever recover. Once
Billaba overcame her wounds,
she took a Padawan named
Caleb Dume. During Order
66, she sacrificed herself on
Kaller to ensure his survival.

Jedi Fellowship

Jedi Master Mace Windu rescued
Billaba from the space pirates who
destroyed her parents. Eventually,
Windu took Billaba as his
Padawan. Over the years, they
have developed a close bond.

DEXTER JETTSTER

BESALISK COOK AND INFORMANT

DATA FILE

AFFILIATION: None
HOMEWORLD: Ojom
SPECIES: Besalisk
HEIGHT: 1.9m (6ft 2in)
APPEARANCES: II
SEE ALSO: Obi-Wan Kenobi

Male Besalisk crest

Powerful arm

Dexterous fingers

Dexter is chief cook and bottle washer in his diner in an unfashionable part of Coruscant.

THE FOUR-ARMED Besalisk named Dexter Jettster runs a diner on Coruscant. Dexter is an individual with diverse connections. This is why Obi-Wan Kenobi seeks him out when he needs information on a mysterious toxic saberdart that has killed assassin Zam Wesell.

THE GRUFF

but good-hearted Dexter Jettster spent many years manning oil rigs across the galaxy, tending bar, brawling, and running weapons on the side. On Coruscant, he has made a fresh start with his diner.

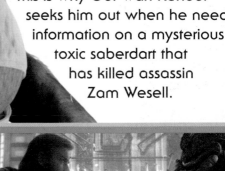

Informant

Beneath his sloppy exterior, Dexter has a keen sense of observation and a retentive memory. He can serve up vital information, even to the likes of a Jedi Knight such as Obi-Wan Kenobi.

DJ

DATA FILE

AFFILIATION: Himself
HOMEWORLD: Unknown
SPECIES: Human
HEIGHT: 1.88m (6ft 2in)
APPEARANCES: VIII
SEE ALSO: Finn; Rose Tico

Badge stamped "Don't Join"

Work boots carried around neck

NOT JUST your average codebreaker, DJ can "slice" into any encrypted computer. Even the First Order's most bio-hexacrypted data systems pose no obstacle for his masterful skills.

DJ USES his knack for cryptography to prey on the wealthy patrons in Canto Bight's casinos. They are arms dealers, war-profiteers, and criminals, so DJ feels no guilt about stealing from them.

Morally Bankrupt

Loyal only to himself, DJ has no qualms about betraying Rose and Finn to the First Order. His mantra is "Don't Join": he thinks that every cause is flawed and he is better off on his own.

DJ offers to help Finn and Rose sneak aboard the First Order's *Supremacy*—for the right price.

Kod'yok leather coat

DOCTOR EVAZAN

MURDEROUS CRIMINAL

DATA FILE

AFFILIATION: Smuggler
HOMEWORLD: Alsakan
SPECIES: Human
HEIGHT: 1.77m (5ft 8in)
APPEARANCES: RO, IV
SEE ALSO: Ponda Baba

Facial scarring

Evazan and Ponda Baba pull blasters: bartender Wuher ducks, but Kenobi stands his ground.

Weapons belt

CARRYING MULTIPLE death sentences, the murderous Doctor Evazan is notorious for rearranging body parts on living creatures. Evazan and his partner, Ponda Baba, also enjoy brawling and gunning down defenseless beings.

Holster

EVAZAN was once a promising surgeon. However, during his training he was corrupted by madness. He now practices "creative surgery" (without the assistance of droids) on hundreds of victims, leaving them hideously scarred.

Criminal Thug

Evazan is a smuggler and murderer with many enemies across the galaxy. A bounty hunter once tried to destroy Evazan, scarring his face. An Aqualish troublemaker named Ponda Baba saved him and became his partner in crime.

DOCTOR KALONIA

RESISTANCE MEDICAL OFFICER

DATA FILE

AFFILIATION: Resistance
HOMEWORLD: Unknown
SPECIES: Human
HEIGHT: 1.73m (5ft 7in)
APPEARANCES: VII
SEE ALSO: Admiral Statura; Chewbacca

DOCTOR HARTER KALONIA'S sympathetic bedside manner and good humor can mend the spirits of wounded Resistance personnel. She is both a skilled doctor and surgeon.

Military rank badge

Medical services armband

Resistance tunic

BASED AT THE Resistance headquarters on D'Qar, Doctor Kalonia makes do with an understaffed medical center. Prior to open conflict with the First Order, Kalonia's main duties involve dealing with the illnesses and exposure that the troops suffer in the exotic climate of the lush planet.

Comfortable boots for long hours spent standing

Medical Chief

Kalonia holds the military rank of major, though she can command greater authority over medical matters, relieving higher-ranking officers of duty if she feels it is necessary. She is also a skilled linguist—her fluency in the Wookiee language, Shyriiwook, helps soothe a nervous Chewbacca after he is wounded.

DROOFY McCOOL

HORN PLAYER IN THE MAX REBO BAND

DATA FILE

AFFILIATION: Jabba's court
HOMEWORLD: Kirdo III
SPECIES: Kitonak
HEIGHT: 1.6m (5ft 3in)
APPEARANCES: VI
SEE ALSO: Jabba the Hutt;
Max Rebo

Tiny eyes hidden by folds of skin

After Jabba's death, McCool disappears into the desert.

Tough, leathery skin

Chidinkalu flute

Body releases a vanilla-like smell

DROOPY McCOOL is the stage name of the lead flute player in the Max Rebo Band, Jabba's house band. A far-out quasi-mystic Kitonak, Droopy's real name is a series of flute-like whistles, unpronounceable by any other species.

MCCOOL is lonely for the company of his own kind and claims to have heard the faint tones of other Kitonaks somewhere out in the Tatooine dunes.

Jamming

Laidback Droopy is largely oblivious to what is going on around him. He hardly recognizes the stage name that Max Rebo gave him—Droopy just plays the tunes.

67

DRYDEN VOS

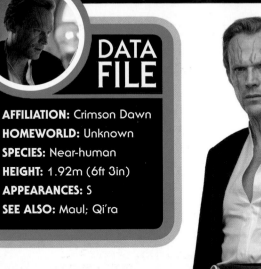

DATA FILE

AFFILIATION: Crimson Dawn
HOMEWORLD: Unknown
SPECIES: Near-human
HEIGHT: 1.92m (6ft 3in)
APPEARANCES: S
SEE ALSO: Maul; Qi'ra

DRYDEN VOS IS THE public face of the vast crime syndicate Crimson Dawn. Few know that its true leader is Maul, the Sith-trained dark-Force user. Vos appears charming, but beware this facade: beneath lurks a vicious thug, who demands nothing less than lifelong loyalty.

Baffleweave cape conceals weapons

Tailored suit made of Pantora silk

A TYRANT in a sharp suit, Vos likes to play the genial host, entertaining the rich and powerful aboard his exquisite star yacht. But his dangerous temper is never far from the surface.

Dryden's luxurious star yacht, filled with priceless antiquities, flaunts his wealth.

Tough Taskmaster

In a brief moment of compassion, Vos gives Tobias Beckett's crew a second chance to bring him coaxium fuel. He allows them to risk their lives with another dangerous mission to acquire some different coaxium— on the understanding that if they fail, then they die.

EETH KOTH

DATA FILE

AFFILIATION: Jedi
HOMEWORLD: Iridonia
SPECIES: Zabrak
HEIGHT: 1.71m (5ft 6in)
APPEARANCES: I, II
SEE ALSO: Mace Windu;
Plo Koon

Vestigial horns

JEDI MASTER AND JEDI High Council member Eeth Koth is an Iridonian Zabrak. This horned species is known for its determination and mental discipline, which enables individuals to tolerate great physical suffering.

Jedi tunic

Traditional leather utility belt

Long, loose robes

DURING the Clone Wars, Eeth Koth is taken hostage by General Grievous. Despite being captured, Koth is able to send a message to the Jedi Council revealing his location. Obi-Wan Kenobi and Adi Gallia stage a daring rescue and successfully retrieve the imprisoned Jedi Master.

Loose sleeves allow freedom of movement

Koth and his fellow Jedi must judge whether Anakin should be trained as a Jedi.

Late Starter

Koth started his Jedi training at the unusually late age of four years, making him more receptive than his fellow council members to Qui-Gon Jinn's appeal to train Anakin Skywalker.

ENFYS NEST

SWOOP-BIKE PIRATE

Transmission antenna

Chromed visor

DATA FILE

AFFILIATION: Cloud-Riders
HOMEWORLD: Unknown
SPECIES: Human
HEIGHT: 1.67m (5ft 5in)
APPEARANCES: S
SEE ALSO: Han Solo

ENFYS NEST is leader of the notorious pirate crew, the Cloud-Riders. From their marauding swoop bikes, this outlaw gang wage war against the Empire as well as crime syndicates like Crimson Dawn.

ENFYS NEST'S fearsome reputation precedes her. An elaborate visor and intimidating outfit hide her true identity. She is known for antics like outwitting and outfighting Tobias Beckett's crew and foiling their attempts to make a living.

Insulating bantha fur

Electroripper staff

From Skyblade-330 swoop bikes, Enfys Nest and the Cloud-Riders can raid starships in midair.

Common Cause

Nest unites those who have lost everything because of the Empire. They use their loot to survive and to fund the fledgling rebel movement.

EV-9D9

SADISTIC DROID SUPERVISOR

DATA FILE

AFFILIATION: Jabba's court
TYPE: Supervisor droid
MANUFACTURER: MerenData
HEIGHT: 1.9m (6ft 2in)
APPEARANCES: VI
SEE ALSO: C-3PO; R2-D2

Degraded logic center

Supervisor

As Jabba's droid overseer, EV-9D9 assigns C-3PO as the Hutt's translator and R2-D2 as drinks waiter on Jabba's sail barge.

Manipulator arm

Custom-fitted third eye

EV-9D9 IS Jabba the Hutt's droid overseer in the murky depths of his palace on Tatooine. EV-9D9's programming is corrupted, and she works Jabba's droids until they fall apart, employing bizarre forms of droid torture to increase motivation.

EV-9D9 IS not the only EV unit with the programming defect that causes her cruel behavior. Many have the same flaw, but EV-9D9 was one of the few to escape the mass recall. EV-9D9 now relishes her role as taskmaster of all droids at the palace.

EV-9D9 added a third eye to herself to "see" droid pain.

EVEN PIELL

LANNIK JEDI MASTER

DATA FILE

AFFILIATION: Jedi
HOMEWORLD: Lannik
SPECIES: Lannik
HEIGHT: 1.22m (4ft)
APPEARANCES: I, II
SEE ALSO: Anakin Skywalker;
Qui-Gon Jinn; Yoda

Jedi topknot

Large ears sensitive in thin atmosphere

Jedi robe

THIS OUTSPOKEN JEDI MASTER is not to be underestimated. Even Piell bears a scar across his eye as a grisly trophy of a victory against terrorists who made the mistake of thinking too little of the undersized Jedi.

PIELL IS from Lannik, a planet with a long history of war. A gruff and battle-hardened warrior during the Clone Wars, Piell is taken prisoner and held captive at the infamous Citadel Station. Though mortally wounded during his escape, he is able to transfer vital information crucial to the war effort to Ahsoka Tano.

Seated next to Yaddle, Even Piell has one of the long-term seats on the Jedi High Council.

Momentous Events

Even Piell sits on the Jedi High Council during the galaxy's first steps toward war. He is present when Qui-Gon Jinn presents the young Anakin Skywalker to the esteemed Jedi leaders for the first time.

FIGRIN D'AN

BITH BAND LEADER

DATA FILE

AFFILIATION: Modal Nodes
HOMEWORLD: Bith
SPECIES: Bith
HEIGHT: 1.79m (5ft 9in)
APPEARANCES: IV
SEE ALSO: Jabba the Hutt

Enlarged cranium

Large eyes

Tone mode selectors

Kloo horn

A Wookiee named Chalmun owns the cantina in which the Modal Nodes often play.

DEMON KLOO horn player Figrin D'an is the frontman for the Modal Nodes, a group of seven Bith musicians. They play in various venues on Tatooine, including Chalmun's Cantina in Mos Eisley and Jabba the Hutt's desert palace.

Band pants

FIGRIN IS a demanding band leader, who expects the best from his musicians. His overbearing nature has earned him the nickname "Fiery" Figrin D'an. As well as playing the kloo horn, Figrin is a compulsive card shark who frequently gambles the band's earnings.

Band Members

The Modal Nodes are Figrin D'an on kloo horn, Doikk Na'ts on Dorenian Beshniquel (or Fizzz), Ickabel G'ont on the Double Jocimer, Tedn Dahai on fanfar, Tech Mo'r on the Ommni Box, Nalan Cheel on the bandfill, and Sun'il Ei'de on the drums. Lirin Car'n often sits in to play second kloo horn.

Travel boots

FINN

STORMTROOPER DESERTER

DATA FILE

AFFILIATION: First Order/ Resistance
HOMEWORLD: Unknown
SPECIES: Human
HEIGHT: 1.78m (5ft 8in)
APPEARANCES: VII, VIII
SEE ALSO: Poe Dameron; Rey; Rose Tico

Finn's inside knowledge about Imperial Star Destroyers proves handy when he, Rose, and DJ infiltrate Snoke's ship to find a tracking device.

Resistance-issue belt

A STORMTROOPER who flees the First Order after a traumatizing first mission, FN-2187 finds a new home—and the name Finn—by joining the Resistance. He risks his life to try to bring down the First Order.

Resistance fighter jacket "borrowed" from Poe Dameron

FN-2187 HAS trained all his life to be an effective stormtrooper. He scored well in combat simulations, but during his first mission, he finds he does not have the brutal instinct to kill innocents in the name of the First Order.

Reckless Escape

Deserting from the First Order ranks, FN-2187 frees a Resistance prisoner, pilot Poe Dameron, who helps the fugitive stormtrooper escape from his Star Destroyer aboard a stolen TIE fighter. Poe gives FN-2187 the name "Finn." Crash-landing on the desert world Jakku, Finn's encounter with a scavenger named Rey will change the course of his life.

FIRST ORDER EXECUTIONER TROOPER

PUNISHERS OF TREASON

AFFILIATION: First Order
TYPE: Human
STANDARD EQUIPMENT:
Laser ax
APPEARANCES: VIII
SEE ALSO: Captain Phasma;
First Order stormtrooper

Vocoder keeps trooper anonymous

Energy ribbon

Carbon-finish armor

DEATH BY BLASTER is sometimes considered too good for someone accused of treason against the First Order. Enter the executioner troopers: a class of stormtrooper equipped for justice by laser ax.

EXECUTIONER DUTY

can fall to any stormtrooper. Four razor-sharp energy ribbons on a laser ax deliver harsh First Order justice in a very public display of force and drama.

Betaplast knee plate

The black section over the dome of a soldier's helmet is the mark of an executioner trooper.

Narrow Escape

Finn made an enemy of Captain Phasma when he deserted her army. Now he is in her custody, along with fellow resistance fighter Rose. Phasma orders two executioner troopers to eliminate them—but Finn and Rose escape when the starship is attacked.

FIRST ORDER FLAMETROOPER

INCENDIARY WEAPONS STORMTROOPERS

DATA FILE

AFFILIATION: First Order
SPECIES: Human
STANDARD EQUIPMENT:
Flame projector
APPEARANCES: VII, VIII
SEE ALSO: First Order
snowtrooper; First Order
stormtrooper

FLAMETROOPERS are specialized stormtroopers of the First Order, who carry weapons that can transform any battlefield into an inferno. The First Order deploys flametroopers during the raid on Tuanul village on Jakku.

Conflagrine tank

D-93w flame projector gun

FLAMETROOPERS

carry D-93 Incinerators, a double-barreled flame projector that sprays an extremely flammable gel—conflagrine-14—from double storage tanks on the trooper's back. After being ignited electrically, the gel can be launched to a distance of 75 meters (246ft).

Flameproof gaiters

Resistance soldier nicknames for flametroopers include "roasters," "hotheads," and "burnouts."

Flames of War

Flametrooper armor is reinforced cyramech that offers protection from heat, and the helmet's slit-visor reduces glare caused by intense flames. Flametroopers work alongside standard stormtroopers to methodically flush enemies out from cover.

FIRST ORDER SNOWTROOPER

COLD WEATHER ASSAULT STORMTROOPERS

DATA FILE

AFFILIATION: First Order
SPECIES: Human
STANDARD EQUIPMENT:
Blaster rifle, blaster pistol
APPEARANCES: VII, VIII
SEE ALSO: First Order
flametrooper; First Order
stormtrooper

The surface glare and crystalline structure of Crait's salt crust are well suited to snowtroopers—if their heating is switched off.

F-11D blaster rifle

AS THE FIRST Order's Starkiller operation is based on an icy planet, base security operations are entrusted to the cold weather divisions of the stormtrooper ranks.

Insulating kama

Utility pouch

SNOWTROOPER ARMOR offers more
mobility than the standard trooper outfit, to make up for the difficulties of snowbound and icy terrain. Insulated fabric covers most of the armor, while a heating and personal environment unit in the trooper's backpack monitors and regulates body temperature.

Ice Warriors

Aside from defending the Starkiller, snowtroopers are tasked with the conquest of icy worlds. The exposed sections of betaplast armor are treated with a de-icing agent that prevents frost buildup. The helmet visor is a minimal slit to reduce ice glare, and heating filaments line essential equipment to prevent freezing.

FIRST ORDER STORMTROOPER

DATA FILE

AFFILIATION: First Order
SPECIES: Human
STANDARD EQUIPMENT:
Blaster rifle, blaster pistol
APPEARANCES: VII, VIII
SEE ALSO: Captain
Phasma; Finn

Rank pauldron

Ammunition container

THE STANDARD INFANTRY
of the First Order purposely
resemble the feared soldiers
of the Old Empire, which in
turn were inspired by the clone
troopers of the Republic.

FIRST ORDER

stormtroopers are trained from
childhood to be soldiers. They
undergo extensive combat drilling.
Detailed simulations ensure a
standard of excellence across
their ranks that far surpasses
that of the Old Empire's
stormtroopers.

The standard weaponry of
the First Order stormtrooper
is the versatile Sonn-Blas
F-11D rifle and the smaller
Sonn-Blas SE-44C pistol.

Improved
joint design

Into Battle

Ten standard infantry stormtroopers form
the basic squad unit. One of those ten
may also be a specialist trooper—a
flametrooper, a stormtrooper equipped
with an FWMB-10 megablaster, or a riot
control stormtrooper.

FIRST ORDER TIE PILOT

LATEST GENERATION PILOTS

Targeting sensors

Complete vac-seal helmet

Life-support gear

DATA FILE

AFFILIATION: First Order
SPECIES: Human
STANDARD EQUIPMENT:
Blaster pistol
APPEARANCES: VII, VIII
SEE ALSO: General Hux;
Poe Dameron

MODERN TIE PILOTS benefit from the First Order's increased focus on the durability and survivability of its forces. This new generation is much better equipped than Imperial ones were.

The standard TIE fighter craft of the First Order is designated the TIE/fo.

WITH NO access to the Empire's former academies, the First Order instead trains its pilots in secret aboard its growing fleets of Star Destroyers. The new generation of TIE pilots spend most of their lives in space.

Positive gravity pressure boots

Special Forces

A subset of the First Order TIE corps are the Special Forces, identifiable by the red markings on their helmets and ships. These are elite pilots who fly a special two-person starfighter with enhanced shields and hyperdrive.

GALEN ERSO

SCIENTIFIC GENIUS

PRIZE-WINNING scientist Galen Erso specializes in crystallography. He wants his research into kyber crystals to help the galaxy recover from the devastating Clone Wars. But without realizing it, he lays the foundations for the most devastating super weapon ever seen—the Death Star.

Research division plaque

Standard Imperial-issue belt buckle

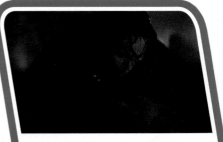

Galen Erso has not seen his daughter since she was eight years old. Jyn finds him on Eadu just in time to say goodbye.

Act of Redemption

Trapped in an Imperial research facility, Erso grapples with the horror of what he has unleashed. He may be unable to stop the construction of the Death Star, but he finds a way to take his revenge: a tiny, hidden flaw that makes the weapon vulnerable to a single shot in the right place. Eventually, he finds a way to get a holomessage to the Rebel Alliance.

GALEN ERSO loved science and wanted it to make the galaxy a better place. He discovers how to get a staggering amount of energy from kyber crystals, but his research is hijacked by the Empire. Director Orson Krennic sees its destructive potential and forces Erso to work for the Empire. Erso's intelligence and knowledge cost him his family, his freedom, and ultimately his life.

Imperial development project uniform

GAMORREAN GUARD

DATA FILE

AFFILIATION: Jabba's court
HOMEWORLD: Gamorr
HEIGHT: 1.7m (5ft 6in)
APPEARANCES: VI
SEE ALSO: Jabba the Hutt

TOUGH, BRUTISH Gamorrean guards stand throughout Jabba's Tatooine palace as sentries. These stocky, slow-witted, green-skinned creatures are stubborn and loyal, though prone to outbursts of barbaric violence.

Weak eyes

Fangs

Gamorreans are willing spectators to the casual violence at Jabba's palace.

Gauntlet

Heavy-duty ax

GAMORREANS

come from the warlike Outer Rim planet Gamorr. Male Gamorreans, called boars, either fight terrible wars or prepare for war, while the female sows farm and hunt.

Gamorreans are tasty treats for Jabba's rancor.

Leather sandals

Fit for Duty

The low intelligence of the Gamorreans makes them almost impossible to bribe, which is an asset to their masters. Their preferred weapons are axes and vibro-lances rather than blasters.

GARINDAN

DATA FILE

AFFILIATION: Various
HOMEWORLD: Kubindi
SPECIES: Kubaz
HEIGHT: 1.85m (6ft 1in)
APPEARANCES: IV
SEE ALSO: Luke Skywalker;
Sandtrooper

GARINDAN IS A greedy and immoral Kubaz from the planet Kubindi. He is a paid informant who works for the highest bidder. In Mos Eisley, the Imperial authorities hire Garindan to locate two missing droids. The lowlife spy quickly picks up the trail of Luke Skywalker, Obi-Wan Kenobi, R2-D2, and C-3PO.

On the Scent

Garindan discovers Luke Skywalker and his friends' plan to meet Han Solo at docking bay 94. Following the group, the sneaky spy then uses his Imperial comlink to call the authorities. When a squad of sandtroopers arrives, Garindan's job is done.

Garindan has a long trunk, which he uses to dine on his favorite delicacy: insects.

Dark goggles

Insect-
eating trunk

THE MYSTERIOUS

Garindan keeps his face hidden behind a dark hood and goggles. Few individuals know anything much about his private life, which is also shrouded in secrecy.

Imperial
comlink

GENERAL DRAVEN

REBEL INTELLIGENCE LEADER

DATA FILE

AFFILIATION: Rebel Alliance
HOMEWORLD: Pendarr III
SPECIES: Human
HEIGHT: 1.91m (6ft 3in)
APPEARANCES: RO
SEE ALSO: Cassian Andor; General Merrick; Princess Leia

Rank pips for General

GENERAL DAVITS DRAVEN is a veteran of the Clone Wars. He now finds himself fighting the Imperial military, which includes many of his former Republic colleagues. Draven represents intelligence on the Rebel Alliance's Yavin base.

Large, practical pockets for field missions

Draven listens in to the Eadu mission. Will Cassian Andor succeed in his covert orders to take out Galen Erso?

DRAVEN is a pragmatic leader who deals in facts, and errs on the side of caution. He regards the intelligence about a Death Star as credible, but thinks its source, Galen Erso, could be a trap. So he does not hesitate in giving orders for Erso to be killed on sight.

Operation Fracture

Draven tries to piece together fragments of information about scientist Galen Erso and the Empire's alleged plans for a superweapon. The mission to find Galen Erso is dubbed "Operation Fracture."

GENERAL EMATT

REBEL VETERAN

DATA FILE

AFFILIATION: Resistance
HOMEWORLD: Unknown
SPECIES: Human
HEIGHT: 1.8m (5ft 9in)
APPEARANCES: VII, VIII
SEE ALSO: Admiral Statura;
C-3PO; Han Solo; Major
Brance; Princess Leia

CALUAN EMATT is a veteran of the Rebel Alliance, and was one of the first officers to join General Leia Organa's cause in the Resistance. He is promoted from major to general to take on the exterior defense of the rebel base on Crait.

Wrist-mounted comms device

Neuro-Saav TE4.4 field quadnoculars

DURING THE Galactic Civil War, Ematt served as leader of the Shrikes. This was a special reconnaissance team responsible for identifying, securing, and preparing new locations to serve as safe zones for the Rebel Alliance.

BlasTech EL-16 blaster rifle

Resistance Recruiter

In the early days of the Resistance, Ematt served as an agent for General Organa. He continued to serve in the New Republic military while seeking out potential converts for Resistance service. After the defection of too many New Republic pilots went unnoticed, Ematt himself left his New Republic post to fully serve the Resistance.

GENERAL GRIEVOUS

COMMANDER OF THE DROID ARMY

DATA FILE

AFFILIATION: Separatists
HOMEWORLD: Kalee
SPECIES: Kaleesh (cyborg)
HEIGHT: 2.16m (7ft 1in)
APPEARANCES: III
SEE ALSO: Count Dooku;
Obi-Wan Kenobi; Palpatine

GENERAL GRIEVOUS is the Supreme Commander of the Droid Army during the Clone Wars. Grievous reacts furiously to any suggestion that he is a droid. In fact, he is a cyborg: a twisted mix of organic body parts and mechanical armor, with a hunched back and a bad cough.

Grievous's end comes when Obi-Wan Kenobi fires blaster bolts at his vulnerable gutsack.

GRIEVOUS IS a Kaleesh warlord who was rebuilt to increase his fighting prowess. The cyborg general is not Force-sensitive, but Darth Tyranus (Count Dooku) trained him in lightsaber combat.

Reptilian eyes

Cape contains pockets for lightsabers

Electro-driven arms can split in half

Prepared for Battle

After their battle during the rescue of Palpatine, Obi-Wan Kenobi faces Grievous again in the Separatist base on Utapau. This time Grievous splits apart his arms in order to wield four lightsabers.

Grievous makes a daring assault on Coruscant in his flagship, the *Invisible Hand*.

GENERAL HUX

DATA FILE

AFFILIATION: First Order
HOMEWORLD: Arkanis
SPECIES: Human
HEIGHT: 1.85m (6ft 1in)
APPEARANCES: VII, VIII
SEE ALSO: Captain Phasma;
Finn; Kylo Ren

A YOUNG, ruthless officer in the First Order, General Hux has total confidence in his troops, training methods, and technology. He relishes unleashing terrifying weapons upon the galaxy and longs to wipe out the Resistance.

Charcoal-gray general's uniform

THE SON OF a prominent Imperial, Hux grew up celebrating the accomplishments of the Old Empire. He, like many in the First Order, believes that the New Republic are unworthy usurpers of power, and that the galaxy must be ruled with a strong hand.

Polished officer's buckle

Hux sees the Starkiller weapon as the ultimate expression of First Order doctrine—dominance through technological might.

Insulated boots

Hux and Kylo

Hux follows Supreme Leader Snoke, and is not happy when Kylo Ren seizes Snoke's place. As a man who believes in data, Hux has little time for the mystical side of the First Order embodied by Ren. But, Hux finds himself helpless against Ren's dark-side power.

GENERAL MADINE

REBEL COMMANDER AND TACTICIAN

DATA FILE

AFFILIATION: Rebel Alliance/
New Republic
HOMEWORLD: Corellia
SPECIES: Human
HEIGHT: 1.7m (5ft 6in)
APPEARANCES: VI
SEE ALSO: Admiral Ackbar;
Mon Mothma

AS COMMANDER of the Rebel Alliance Special Forces, General Madine devises the plan to destroy the Imperial shield generator on Endor's Moon. He also trains the strike force that infiltrates the Moon.

Command insignia

Rebel uniform jerkin

Briefing documents

Military gauntlets

General Madine helps Admiral Ackbar direct the Battle of Endor from the rebel flagship.

CRIX MADINE

led an Imperial commando unit until his defection to the Rebel Alliance. He is an expert in small ground strikes. Madine's unit of Alliance commandos was responsible for the capture of Imperial equipment and intelligence vital to crucial Alliance operations.

Rebel Advisor

Madine is a respected advisor to the rebel leader Mon Mothma. Before the Battle of Endor, Madine and Mothma brief their troops on board the Rebel Headquarters frigate, *Home One*. After the fall of the Empire, Madine commands the New Republic Special Forces.

BLUE LEADER AT THE BATTLE OF SCARIF

Koensayr
K-22995 helmet

DATA FILE

AFFILIATION: Rebel Alliance
HOMEWORLD: Virujansi
SPECIES: Human
HEIGHT: 1.82m (6ft)
APPEARANCES: RO
SEE ALSO: Admiral Raddus; General Draven

GENERAL ANTOC MERRICK

commands all the starfighter groups on the rebel Massassi base on the moon Yavin 4. An adept pilot himself, he leads Blue Squadron from his T-65B X-wing starfighter at the Battle of Scarif.

Atmosphere exchange hose

Guidenhauser ejection harness

GENERAL Merrick commands the X-wing, Y-wing, and U-wing pilots on Yavin 4. One of only a few pilots who have been Blue Leader, Merrick flies—for the first and last time—under the "Blue One" call sign at the Battle of Scarif.

Caring Commander

Unlike General Draven, who orders his troops with a cold pragmatism, Merrick puts his pilots first. He would never risk lives needlessly, though he does not hesitate to scramble troops when needed. He particularly thinks highly of U-wing pilots who put themselves in the most dangerous line of fire in order to deliver ground troops.

As well as flying missions, General Merrick has a voice on the Rebel Council.

GENERAL RIEEKAN

REBEL COMMANDER OF ECHO BASE

DATA FILE

AFFILIATION: Rebel Alliance
HOMEWORLD: Alderaan
SPECIES: Human
HEIGHT: 1.8m (5ft 9in)
APPEARANCES: V
SEE ALSO: Princess Leia

GENERAL CARLIST RIEEKAN is in charge of Echo Base on Hoth. He keeps the seven hidden levels of the base in a state of constant alert, ever wary of discovery by Imperial forces. Rieekan knows that any rebel activity could be easy to detect in the frozen Hoth system.

Rebel command insignia

RIEEKAN was born on Alderaan, Leia Organa's adopted planet. He fought for the Republic in the Clone Wars and became a founding member of the Rebel Alliance. Rieekan is off-world when the Death Star superweapon destroys Alderaan, but this terrible event will haunt the rebel commander ever after.

Rieekan waits until all other rebel transports have left Hoth before escaping himself.

Utility belt

Insulated rebel uniform jacket

Command gauntlet

Stern Leader

Carlist Rieekan is a decisive commander. When the Imperial army discovers Echo Base, Rieekan plans to delay Vader's forces long enough to give the rebels time to evacuate the base.

GENERAL VEERS

IMPERIAL COMMANDER ON HOTH

DATA FILE

AFFILIATION: Empire
HOMEWORLD: Denon
SPECIES: Human
HEIGHT: 1.93m (6ft 3in)
APPEARANCES: V
SEE ALSO:
Admiral Ozzel;
Admiral Piett

GENERAL MAXIMILIAN VEERS is cunning and capable. He has rapidly worked his way up the Imperial ranks. A family man, Veers is viewed as a model Imperial officer.

Blast helmet

Pilot armor

Utility belt contains mission data

Imperial officer's uniform

GENERAL VEERS

is the mastermind behind the devastating Imperial assault on Echo Base—the Rebel Alliance base on Hoth. He commands the Empire's attack in person from within the cockpit of the lead AT-AT, codenamed *Blizzard One.*

General Veers takes aim at the rebels from inside the cockpit of his AT-AT.

Cruel Ambition

Desperate to prove himself to Darth Vader, Veers heads the AT-AT regiment that successfully destroys the rebel shield power generator, allowing Vader to land on Hoth. Imperial snowtroopers, armed with heavy weapons, then infiltrate Echo Base with frightening speed.

GEONOSIAN SOLDIER

SPECIALIZED GEONOSIAN DRONES

DATA FILE

AFFILIATION: Separatists
HOMEWORLD: Geonosis
SPECIES: Geonosian
HEIGHT: 1.7m (5ft 6in)
APPEARANCES: II
SEE ALSO: Count Dooku;
Poggle the Lesser

Prongs protect
vulnerable blood vessels

Powerful
sonic blaster

GEONOSIAN SOLDIER
drones are tough and
single-minded. They
are trained to fight with
a fearless attitude and
are effective against brute
opponents. However, they
are poor attackers when
faced with intelligent
enemies.

SOLDIER drones are grown
to adulthood rapidly, and can be
ready for combat at an age of
only six years. They carry sonic
blasters, which produce a
devastating sonic ball.

Soldier drones
can fly or hover

Well-developed
soldier's thigh

Geonosians once numbered
in the billions. They were
practically wiped out after
the completion of a secret
Imperial construction project.

Red iketa
stone traditionally
associated with war

Like Geonosian blasters, the
LR1K cannons rely upon
sonic-based attacks.

Segregation

The caste-segregated planet Geonosis has
become the chief supplier of battle droids
to the Separatists, led by the aristocratic
Count Dooku. Huge factories on Geonosis
churn out countless droids.

GRAND MOFF TARKIN

ARCHITECT OF THE DEATH STAR

DATA FILE

AFFILIATION:
Republic/Empire
HOMEWORLD: Eriadu
SPECIES: Human
HEIGHT: 1.82m (6ft)
APPEARANCES: III, RO, IV
SEE ALSO: Orson Krennic;
Palpatine

AT THE END of the Clone Wars, Wilhuff Tarkin already has an exalted position as one of Palpatine's regional governors. As Grand Moff Tarkin, he plans the horrific Death Star as part of his doctrine of Rule by Fear.

Tarkin dies on the Death Star when rebel X-wings cause it to self-destruct.

Code cylinder

TARKIN has a history of quelling rebellion by the most cold-blooded means. He also created the role of Grand Moff—an official who has responsibility for stamping out trouble in "priority sectors" across the Empire.

Imperial officer's disk

Rule by Fear

In order to force Princess Leia to betray the Rebel Alliance, Tarkin orders the destruction of Alderaan by the Death Star. Rather than attempting to police all the scattered individual systems in the Imperial Outlands, Tarkin believes that fear of the Death Star will subjugate systems across the galaxy.

The Death Star project, led by Orson Krennic, is named the Tarkin Initiative.

GREEATA

PERFORMER IN THE MAX REBO BAND

DATA FILE

AFFILIATION: Jabba's court
HOMEWORLD: Rodia
SPECIES: Rodian
HEIGHT: 1.7m (5ft 6in)
APPEARANCES: III, VI
SEE ALSO: Lyn Me; Max Rebo; Rystáll; Sy Snootles

Antennae detect vibrations

Flamboyant hairstyle decorated with feathers

GREEATA JENDOWANIAN is a backup singer, dancer, and musician in the Max Rebo Band in Jabba's desert palace. Greeata forms a colorful alien trio with Rystáll Sant and Lyn Me.

Dancing costume

Pheromone-suppressing bracelet

Suction-tipped fingers

GREEATA'S love of music and dance began as a youngster on her home planet of Rodia. She started out playing the kloo horn, and took a job on board a luxury liner, where she met fellow singer Sy Snootles. Together they formed a performing duo, which Max Rebo spotted playing in a cantina.

Singing for Hutts

Rystáll Sant, Greeata, and Lyn Me perform together at Jabba's palace. Graceful and rhythmic dancers make a powerful impression on the heavy, slow-moving Hutts. All the performers compete for Jabba's favor and indulgence.

Jabba's palace on Tatooine is hidden away in the Western Dune Sea.

GREEDO

RODIAN BOUNTY HUNTER

DATA FILE

AFFILIATION: Bounty hunter
HOMEWORLD: Rodia
SPECIES: Rodian
HEIGHT: 1.73m (5ft 7in)
APPEARANCES: IV
SEE ALSO: Han Solo;
Jabba the Hutt

Head spikes

Large eyes see in
infrared spectrum

GREEDO IS A RODIAN bounty hunter who works for Jabba the Hutt. During the Clone Wars, he kidnaps Baron Papanoida's daughters, Che Amanwe and Chi Eekway. When Greedo demands debt payment from Han Solo in a Mos Eisley cantina, he finally meets his match.

GREEDO grew up on Tatooine and was known for his temper. He sometimes attempted to start fights with others, including Anakin Skywalker, who was then a slave in Mos Espa.

Blaster pistol

Well-worn
flightsuit

Long,
dexterous
fingers

Greedo's End

The confrontation that takes place in the crowded cantina between Greedo and Han Solo begins with Greedo pulling a blaster on Solo. When Solo claims not to have the money on him, there is an exchange of blaster fire—and the Rodian falls dead on the table. Solo leaves, tossing a few coins at the bartender to hush up the incident.

GRUMMGAR

BIG GAME HUNTER

A MERCENARY and big game hunter, Grummgar is obsessed with trophies. His bulky frame supports an enormous ego, and he does not realize that his partner, Bazine Netal, is a spy working him for information.

Hunting Grounds

Grummgar frequents Maz Kanata's castle, looking for hunting tips from the explorers who ply Wild Space and the Unknown Regions. Scouts' stories describing untamed worlds teeming with predators fill him with joy, and he returns from hunting expeditions with tales as tall as he is.

Plastoid armor plate

THOUGH unscrupulous, Grummgar avoids hunting intelligent prey—he prefers stalking wild animals to being a bounty hunter That said, he will happily trample any rules that prevent poaching, and more than once he has pursued endangered animals on sacred grounds in pursuit of a rare trophy.

GUAVIAN SECURITY SOLDIER

ELITE CRIMINAL ENFORCERS

DATA FILE

AFFILIATION: Guavian Death Gang
SPECIES: Modified human
STANDARD EQUIPMENT: Percussive cannon
APPEARANCES: VII
SEE ALSO: Bala-Tik; Kanjiklub gang

Central sensor and broadcasting dish

Gorget armor

Percussive cannon

THE CYBERNETICALLY enhanced security soldiers of the Guavian Death Gang wear high-impact armor that makes them stand out among other deadly criminals. They are faceless, voiceless killers who show no mercy.

THESE MASKED soldiers communicate using high frequency signals that transmit from the disk in their faceplate. They are otherwise silent, giving them an even greater air of menace.

Ammunition pouch

Flexible armor shin guard

Illegal and Inhuman

A mechanical reservoir worn on the security soldier's leg acts as a second heart, injecting a secret mixture of chemicals that boost a Guavian's speed and aggressiveness. Coupled with the black market prototype weapons carried by the soldiers, everything about them is unnatural and dangerous.

HAN SOLO

SMUGGLER AND WAR HERO

DATA FILE

AFFILIATION: Rebel Alliance/Resistance
HOMEWORLD: Corellia
SPECIES: Human
HEIGHT: 1.8m (5ft 9in)
APPEARANCES: S, IV, V, VI, VII
SEE ALSO: Chewbacca; Princess Leia; Qi'ra

As legend has it, Han Solo is said to have flown the infamous Kessel Run in just under 12 parsecs.

Nerf leather jacket

HAN SOLO IS A pirate, smuggler, and mercenary. With his loyal first mate, Chewbacca, he flies one of the fastest ships in the galaxy—the *Millennium Falcon*. Han is reckless at times, but he proves himself a natural leader in the Rebel Alliance.

CHANGE is a constant in Solo's life. As a young man, he believed he made his own luck and was a man of few responsibilities. As he grows older and wiser, he has difficulty settling down to a life of peace. After suffering personal tragedy, Han once again returns to a reckless life in the criminal underworld.

Strike Force

Han Solo leads a group of rebels, including Chewbacca and Leia, in a risky mission on Endor's moon to destroy the second Death Star's shield generator. Solo shows Leia that there is more to being a scoundrel than having a checkered past!

Action boots

HOTH REBEL TROOPER

DATA FILE

AFFILIATION: Rebel Alliance
SPECIES: Human
STANDARD EQUIPMENT:
Tripod-mounted blasters;
thermal flak jackets;
anti-glare goggles
APPEARANCES: V
SEE ALSO: Rebel trooper

Anti-glare goggles

Thermal flak jacket

Binoculars

Rebel troops use tripod-mounted blasters at the Battle of Hoth.

REBEL SOLDIERS ARE a ragtag bunch. Some are deserters from the Imperial forces, but many more are young volunteers with little or no experience in combat. New recruits receive basic training in handling weapons, communications, and emergency medical relief.

REBEL troopers on the ice planet Hoth must adapt quickly to freezing temperatures and the constant risk of sudden evacuation. They are equipped with specialist snow gear, including thermal flak jackets and polarized anti-glare goggles.

Relocation

After the Battle of Yavin, the Alliance relocates its secret headquarters to Hoth. Anticipating an Imperial invasion, the rebels modify their weapons to function in the icy temperatures.

IG-88

HIDEOUS ASSASSIN DROID

DATA FILE

AFFILIATION: Bounty hunter
TYPE: Assassin droid
MANUFACTURER: Holowan Laboratories
HEIGHT: 1.96m (6ft 5in)
APPEARANCES: V
SEE ALSO: Boba Fett; Darth Vader

Heat sensor

Vocoder

Ammunition bandolier

IG-88 IS A HEAVILY armed assassin droid that offers his services to Darth Vader to capture the *Millennium Falcon* after the Battle of Hoth. Also known as a Phlutdroid, IG-88 is a mechanical droid that has earned a reputation as a merciless hunter.

IG-88 is obsessed with hunting and destroying, as a result of his incompletely formed droid programming. The IG-series was designed to have blasters built into each arm, but they were never installed.

A wrecked IG-88 droid is left for scrap in Cloud City after Boba Fett caught it trailing him.

Outlaws

IG-88 joins the motley assortment of human, alien, and droid bounty hunters on the deck of Darth Vader's ship, the *Executor*. IG-88 and Boba Fett are longtime rivals. Assassin droids like IG-88 were outlawed after the Clone Wars, but they continue to stalk the galaxy.

Pulse cannon

Acid-proof servo wires

IMPERIAL RED GUARD

PALPATINE'S SECURITY FORCE

DATA FILE

AFFILIATION: Republic/ Empire
HEIGHT: 1.83m (6ft)
APPEARANCES: II, III, VI, RO
SEE ALSO: Darth Vader; Palpatine

Full-face helmet with darkened visor

Red Guards eventually come to replace the blue-robed guards of the Galactic Senate.

Force pike

Synthetic leather combat gloves

Long robe conceals hidden weapons

ROYAL, OR RED, Guards are Emperor Palpatine's personal bodyguards. From the moment of his appointment to Supreme Chancellor, these Guards have accompanied Palpatine at all times.

Confrontation

When Moff Jerjerrod and two Red Guards attempt to deny Darth Vader entrance to the Emperor's throne room on the second Death Star, Vader Force-chokes the officer, though not fatally.

RED GUARDS

use vibro-active force pikes, which inflict precise and lethal wounds. Palpatine keeps the details of the Guards' training in deadly arts a secret, citing "security concerns."

JABBA THE HUTT

NOTORIOUS CRIME LORD

DATA FILE

AFFILIATION: Hutt Grand Council, Crymorah Syndicate
HOMEWORLD: Tatooine
SPECIES: Hutt
LENGTH: 3.9m (12ft 8in)
APPEARANCES: I, IV, VI
SEE ALSO: Bib Fortuna; Salacious Crumb

THE REPELLENT CRIME LORD Jabba the Hutt commands an extensive criminal empire. He built his operation through a long history of deals, threats, extortion, murders, and good business sense. Now, Jabba lives a life of wickedness in his palace located on the remote desert world of Tatooine.

Princess Leia exacts the revenge that all Jabba's slaves have dreamed about.

Hutt skin secretes oil and mucus

Muscular body can move like a snail

Body has no skeleton

Ruler

Sitting on his throne, with his slaves and sycophants all around, Jabba presides over a court of murderous depravity. Many bounty hunters and hired thugs seek work here.

JABBA REIGNS as head of the Hutt Grand Council, one of the largest criminal empires in the galaxy. Jabba prefers Tatooine to Nal Hutta, so Gardulla the Hutt often serves as his representative on the council. During the Clone Wars, Jabba allows the Republic to use private Hutt hyperspace lanes in exchange for rescuing his son, Rotta, from kidnappers.

JAN DODONNA

DATA FILE

AFFILIATION: Rebel Alliance
HOMEWORLD: Commenor
SPECIES: Human
HEIGHT: 1.83m (6ft)
APPEARANCES: RO, IV
SEE ALSO: Luke Skywalker;
Mon Mothma; Princess Leia

GENERAL JAN DODONNA is a master tactician for the Rebel Alliance. He commands the assault on the Death Star in the Battle of Yavin. Dodonna identifies the supposedly invulnerable station's single flaw: a small thermal exhaust port that leads straight to the explosive main reactor.

JAN DODONNA

offers his skill and expertise to the Alliance once the Empire comes to power. After the Battle of Yavin, Dodonna is instrumental in locating a new base for the Rebellion.

Rebel tactician's uniform

Ground Support

During the strike on the Death Star, Dodonna provides the rebel pilots with ground support from Yavin. His strategy enables a fleet of 30 fighters to destroy a battle station over 160 kilometers (100 miles) wide.

General Dodonna briefs the rebel pilots in the command room at the rebel base on Yavin 4.

JANGO FETT

CLONE TROOPER TEMPLATE

DATA FILE

AFFILIATION: Bounty hunter, Separatists
HOMEWORLD: Unknown
SPECIES: Human
HEIGHT: 1.83m (6ft)
APPEARANCES: II
SEE ALSO: Boba Fett

Eye sensor allows Jango to see behind him

Segmented armor plate allows flexibility

Fett is an expert pilot and teaches his son, Boba, from an early age.

DESPITE HAVING no affiliation with Mandalore, Jango Fett wears the armored uniform that helped make the Mandalorians a dreaded name. During the Republic's final years, he is regarded as the best bounty hunter in the galaxy.

Gauntlet projectile dart shooter

Fett in his ship, *Slave I*, blasts Obi-Wan Kenobi's Jedi starfighter in the Geonosis asteroid field.

Segmented armor plate

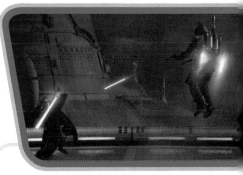

Lethal Opponent

In battle with Obi-Wan Kenobi, Fett launches himself into the air using his jetpack. He carries many weapons, including knee-pad rocket launchers, and wrist gauntlets that fire darts, whipcords, and blades.

FETT'S REPUTATION as a supreme warrior led the Kaminoans to recruit him for their secret army project: every clone trooper is a clone of him. Fett receives a lucrative amount of credits, but also requests one unaltered clone to raise as his son.

JAR JAR BINKS

DATA FILE

AFFILIATION: Gungan Grand Army, Republic
HOMEWORLD: Naboo
SPECIES: Gungan
HEIGHT: 1.96m (6ft 4in)
APPEARANCES: I, II, III
SEE ALSO: Padmé Amidala; Qui-Gon Jinn

Haillu (earlobes) for display

JAR JAR BINKS is an amphibious Gungan from Naboo. During the invasion of Naboo, Jedi Qui-Gon Jinn runs into and rescues Jar Jar. Jar Jar becomes a general in the Gungan Grand Army, and then a Junior Representative in the Galactic Senate.

At first, clumsy Jar Jar proves more of a hindrance than a help at the Battle of Naboo.

During the Clone Wars, Jar Jar goes on many diplomatic missions to aid the Republic.

Cast-off stretchy Gungan pants

Powerful calf muscles for swimming

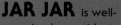

JAR JAR is well-meaning but accident-prone. This simple soul is elevated to a position in the Senate that may be beyond his abilities. Luckily for him, the Naboo value purity of heart over other qualifications to govern.

Tight trouser ends keep out swamp crawlies

Good Intentions

In Padmé's absence, Jar Jar represents Naboo in the Senate. With the best of intentions, he sets in motion a new galactic era as he proposes a motion for Supreme Chancellor Palpatine to accept emergency powers to deal with the Separatist threat.

JAWA

ROBED METAL MERCHANTS

DATA FILE

AFFILIATION: None
HOMEWORLD: Tatooine
HEIGHT: 1m (3ft 3in)
APPEARANCES: I, II, IV, VI
SEE ALSO: R2-D2; Tusken Raider

Heavy hoods protect from sun glare

Glowing eyes

Bandolier

Ionization blaster

JAWAS SCAVENGE scrap metal, lost droids, and equipment on Tatooine. When Jawas arrive to sell and trade at the edge of town, droids stay away and individuals watch their landspeeders extra closely. Things tend to disappear when Jawas are around!

TIMID, GREEDY

Jawas wear dark robes to protect them from Tatooine's twin suns. Their glowing eyes help them see in the dark crevices where they hide, and their rodent-like faces are remarkably ugly to non-Jawas.

Most Jawas patrol the dunes and dusty rocks in gigantic sandcrawlers.

Desert Find

Unlucky droids that wander off or get thrown out as junk are favorite targets for the Jawas. They carry any finds to their sandcrawlers, where a magnetic suction tube draws the captured droid into the bowels of these ancient mining vehicles.

JESS PAVA

DATA FILE

AFFILIATION: Resistance
HOMEWORLD: Dandoran
SPECIES: Human
HEIGHT: 1.69m (5ft 6in)
APPEARANCES: VII
SEE ALSO: Nien Nunb; Poe Dameron; Snap Wexley

A YOUNG, brave pilot, Jess "Testor" Pava serves as Blue Three within the Resistance. She flies alongside Snap Wexley and Poe Dameron in the crucial mission against the First Order Starkiller weapon.

Insulated helmet

Inflatable flight vest

Color known as "Interstellar orange"

THE MASSIVELY

understaffed Resistance requires each member to fill multiple roles. In addition to serving as a pilot, Jess also helps catalog the astromech droids at the D'Qar base.

Ejection harness

Tales of Legends

Like many in the Resistance, Jess idolizes the legendary pilots of the previous generation. She bravely flies into battle above the Starkiller, and, following in the footsteps of the rebel pilots of old, volunteers to continue the mission even in the face of overwhelming First Order defenses.

JYN ERSO

INDEPENDENT REBEL

DATA FILE

AFFILIATION: Formerly part of Saw Gerrera's insurgents
HOMEWORLD: Vallt
SPECIES: Human
HEIGHT: 1.6m (5ft 3in)
APPEARANCES: RO
SEE ALSO: Cassian Andor; Galen Erso; Lyra Erso; Saw Gerrera

EVERYONE IMPORTANT in Jyn Erso's life has abandoned her. It has always been for her own protection, but that is not much comfort. As a result, she is used to relying only on herself and she has become defiant and mistrusting of everyone.

Insulated mechanic's vest

YOUNG AND ALONE,

Jyn learned to survive by herself in a harsh world by using her criminal wits. As she grows, she builds up her resilience with hand-to-hand combat, target practice, and fighting with improvised weapons. She lashes out at the Empire whenever she can.

Stolen weapon

Hardwearing, practical clothes

Jyn has always been ready to run away. She has to leave her family when she is just eight years old.

Unlikely Recruit

The Rebel Alliance need Jyn's help, but they do not trust each other. If her interests align with theirs, she will cooperate—but only on her own terms.

K-2SO

REPROGRAMMED IMPERIAL SECURITY DROID

DATA FILE

AFFILIATION: Alliance Intelligence
TYPE: KX-series security droid
MANUFACTURER: Arakyd Industries
HEIGHT: 2.16m (7ft 1in)
APPEARANCES: RO
SEE ALSO: Cassian Andor; Jyn Erso

Imperial mark

K-2SO HAS THE body of an Imperial security droid, which makes him an alarming sight wandering around a rebel base. Programming is everything though, and since being rewired by Cassian Andor, he is loyal to the Rebellion.

Access door for primary programming port

Articular ring joint

HAVING YOUR

inner circuits prodded and reprogrammed is not without its side effects. K-2SO is now quick to speak his mind—however rude or inappropriate it is—and will not follow orders that he thinks are boring.

K-2SO still has enough Imperial knowledge to find the Death Star files in the vault on Scarif.

Imperial Imposter

K-2SO does not need to steal an Imperial uniform to blend in on Scarif, like Jyn and Cassian have to. He can freely walk off the stolen Imperial cargo shuttle and roam around the secure facility, because he looks just like every other security droid.

KANJIKLUB GANG

FRONTIER BANDITS

DATA FILE

AFFILIATION: Kanjiklub
SPECIES: Human
STANDARD EQUIPMENT:
Cobbled together
blaster weaponry
APPEARANCES: VII
SEE ALSO: Razoo Qin-Fee;
Tasu Leech

THE KANJIKLUB are inhabitants of the planet Nar Kanji who were once enslaved by the Hutt crime lords, but then rebelled and killed their oppressors. They are notorious bandits and pirates.

Boiler rifle

Padded armor

VOLZANG LI-THRULL carries a
Tibanna-jacked boiler rifle
—an overpowered blaster
rifle that uses an explosive
mixture of Tibanna gas to
double its firepower. It is
a dangerous and illegal
modification.

Weapons
concealed in
leg pouches

Deadly Fighters

During their enslavement by the Hutts, the people of Nar Kanji developed martial arts that used improvised weaponry. The modern Kanjiklubbers celebrate this history by outfitting themselves with modified armor and weapons. These gangsters are not to be taken lightly, as Han Solo discovers when he becomes deeply indebted to them.

KI-ADI-MUNDI

CEREAN JEDI MASTER

DATA FILE

AFFILIATION: Jedi
HOMEWORLD: Cerea
SPECIES: Cerean
HEIGHT: 1.98m (6ft 5in)
APPEARANCES: I, II, III
SEE ALSO: Yoda

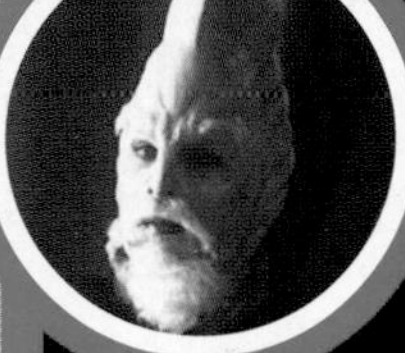

Large brain supported by second heart
Cerean cuffs
Travel pouch
Cerean fighting boots

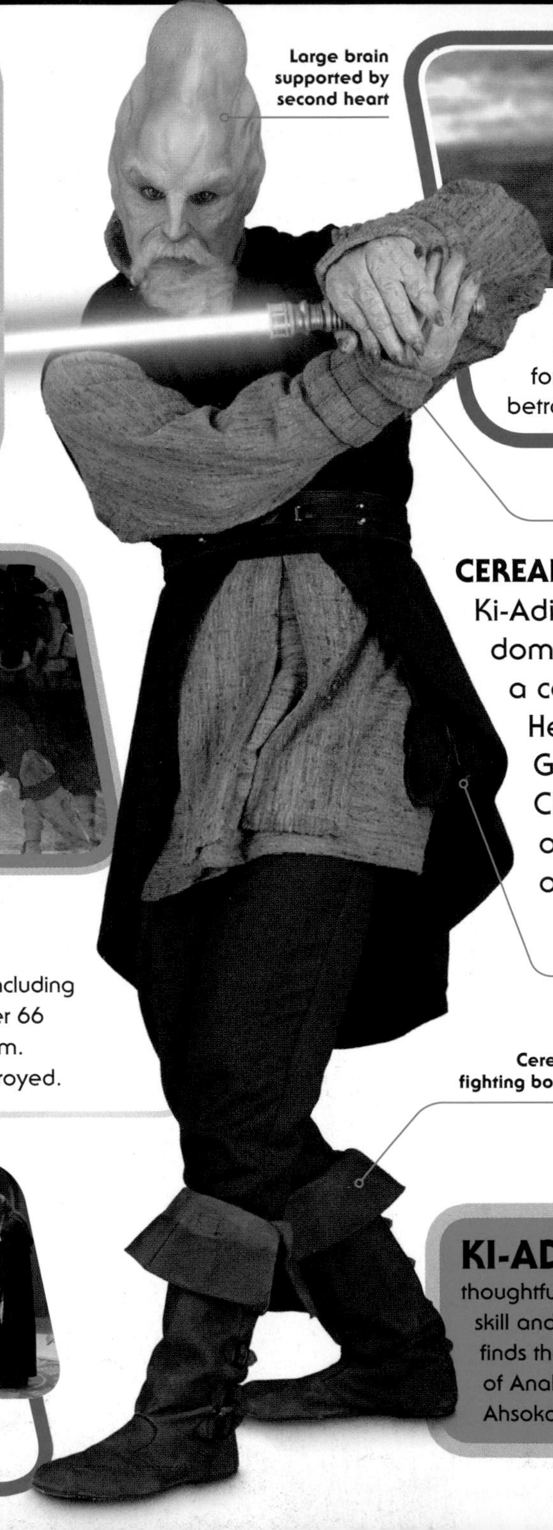

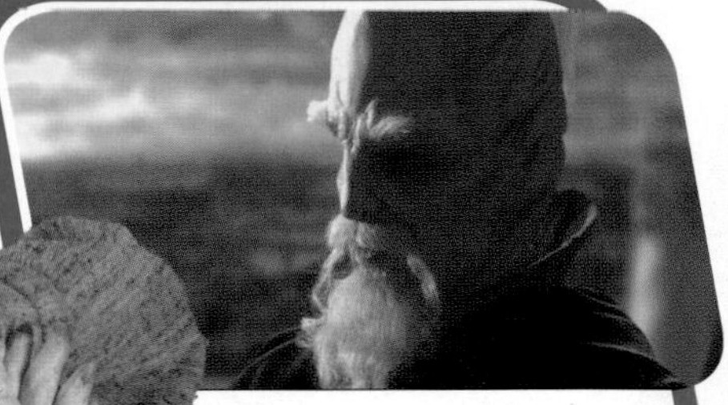

Logical and methodical, Ki-Adi-Mundi cannot foresee the unthinkable betrayal in store for the Jedi.

CEREAN JEDI MASTER

Ki-Adi-Mundi has a high-domed head, which holds a complex binary brain. He becomes a Jedi General during the Clone Wars and fights on Geonosis, among other worlds.

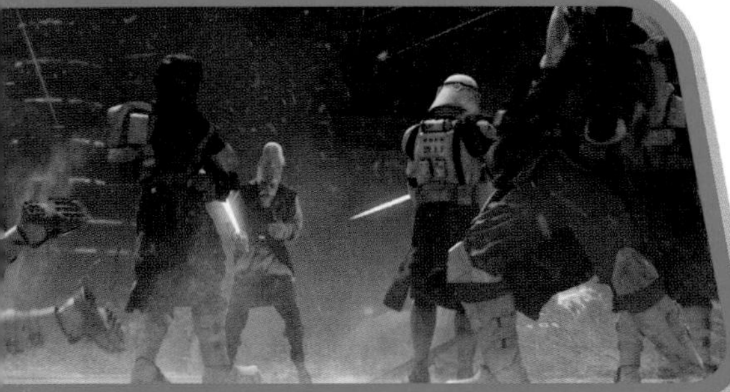

Into Battle

Ki-Adi-Mundi fights alongside Clone Commander Bacara in many battles, including the attack on Mygeeto. But when Order 66 is activated, the clone troops turn on him. He defends himself bravely, but is destroyed.

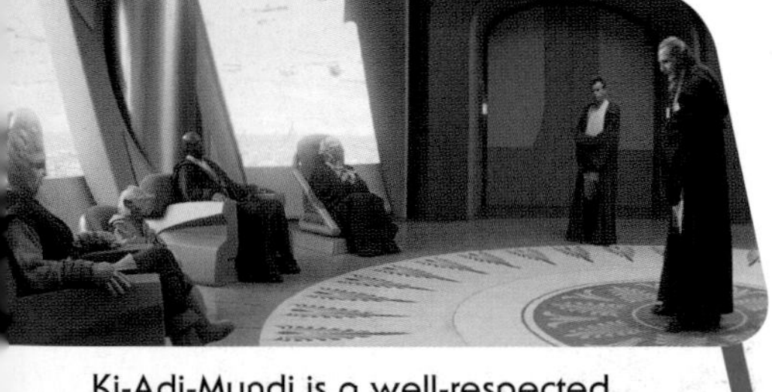

Ki-Adi-Mundi is a well-respected member of the Jedi High Council.

KI-ADI-MUNDI is a thoughtful Jedi who shows great skill and courage in battle. He finds the adventurous nature of Anakin Skywalker and Ahsoka Tano unusual.

KIT FISTO

NAUTOLAN JEDI MASTER

JEDI MASTER KIT FISTO is a fierce fighter who joins the 200 Jedi that travel to Geonosis to rescue the captives from the deadly execution arena. During the Clone Wars, Fisto accepts a seat on the Jedi High Council and is a veteran of many campaigns.

Low-light vision eyes

Tentacles detect chemical signatures

AS AN amphibious Nautolan from Glee Anselm, Kit Fisto can live in air or water. His head tentacles are highly sensitive and allow him to detect others' emotions. This ability allows Fisto to take instant advantage of an opponent's uncertainty in combat.

Jedi robe

Fallen Jedi

Most Jedi are deployed on distant worlds, but Mace Windu manages to assemble a trio of celebrated Jedi, including Kit Fisto, to assist him in arresting Palpatine. However, few Jedi of Mace's generation have fought a Sith Lord, and Fisto falls to Sidious' blade.

Kit Fisto leads a special unit of clone troopers at the Battle of Geonosis.

KORR SELLA

EMISSARY TO THE NEW REPUBLIC

DATA FILE

AFFILIATION: Resistance
HOMEWORLD: Unknown
SPECIES: Human
HEIGHT: 1.65m (5ft 4in)
APPEARANCES: VII
SEE ALSO: Admiral Ackbar;
Admiral Statura; Major
Brance; Princess Leia

LEIA ORGANA'S confrontational approach toward the First Order has left her politically isolated. She relies on emissaries like Korr Sella for continued contact with the New Republic government.

Rank of commander

Resistance officer uniform

DRESSED IN THE uniform of a Resistance officer, Korr Sella is an uncomfortable reminder to New Republic pacifists that war is sometimes inevitable. Leia Organa's words of warning regarding the First Order have caused the New Republic to brand her a warmonger.

Confident stance

Voice of the Resistance

Korr Sella is the daughter of New Republic politicians, but came to believe in Leia Organa's cause. A skilled diplomat, Korr maintains a fragile channel of communication between the Senate and the Resistance. When circumstances look most dire, Leia sends Sella to the Republic capital on Hosnian Prime to ask the New Republic for help.

KYLO REN

DARK SIDE ENFORCER

DATA FILE

AFFILIATION: Knights of Ren/First Order
HOMEWORLD: Chandrila
SPECIES: Human
HEIGHT: 1.89m (6ft 2in)
APPEARANCES: VII, VIII
SEE ALSO: Han Solo; Luke Skywalker; Rey

Unstable plasma blade matrix

A DARK-ROBED warrior strong with the Force, Kylo Ren commands First Order missions with a temper as fiery and barely contained as the power within his lightsaber.

Kylo Ren greatly admires Darth Vader. He owns the Dark Lord's charred and melted helmet.

THOUGH REN can use the Force, he is no Jedi or Sith. He follows his own path, encouraged by Supreme Leader Snoke to use the heritage of both the light and dark sides. These contradictory disciplines create a great conflict within Kylo Ren.

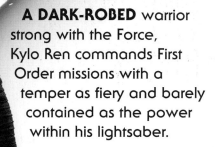

Top Job

Like many apprentices before him, Ren strikes down his master to make way for his own ambitions. With Snoke dead, he declares himself the new Supreme Leader of the First Order. He immediately sets to wiping out the Resistance with renewed vigor and intense rage.

L3-37

PILOT AND SUPPORTER OF DROID RIGHTS

Basic R3
astromech
brain module

PART-ASTROMECH, part-protocol droid, L3-37 has customized her body over time into a mishmash of droid parts. Her personality has also evolved. Unlike standard droids, she not only thinks for herself, but ponders the deep philosophical questions of life.

Ventilation port

Systems are not factory tested so are temperamental

L3-37 IS an exceptional pilot who flies the *Millennium Falcon* with Lando Calrissian. Without her, Han Solo's team would never have reached the speeds and made the hyperspace jumps required to complete the hazardous Kessel Run in 12 parsecs.

Power cell

L3-37 connects to the freighter's navicomputer to plot fast routes for the *Millennium Falcon*.

Droid Liberator

L3-37 wants all droids to enjoy the free will that she has. She speaks out for droid independence and liberates those she can, whether in the droid fighting pits on Vandor or in the refineries of Kessel.

LADY PROXIMA

WHITE WORMS MATRIARCH

DATA FILE

AFFILIATION: White Worms
HOMEWORLD: Corellia
SPECIES: Grindalid
HEIGHT: 4.88m (16ft)
APPEARANCES: S
SEE ALSO: Han Solo;
Moloch; Qi'ra

LADY PROXIMA is a colossal, worm-like creature and matriarch of the White Worms gang that runs Corellia's black market. Poor human children called scrumrats work for her, picking pockets and hunting for vermin to feed her baby Grindalid hatchlings.

Ornamental armored plates

Skin evolved on the Grindalid home planet, which has a dense atmosphere that filters out most light

Grindalid skin burns in sunlight. Han Solo throws a rock through the dark glass of a window, and the sun's rays cause Lady Proxima's skin to blister.

Weak legs

Scrumrats

Han Solo and Qi'ra grow up on Corellia. They fall in with the White Worms and rise to become more senior scrumrats with responsibilities beyond petty crime. However, one day they revolt against Lady Proxima and Han succeeds in not just escaping the gang, but the entire planet of Corellia.

LADY PROXIMA

never ventures outside—scrumrats do that for her. She runs her operations from a network of sewers under Coronet City. In this underworld, she spends most of her time Immersed in a briny pool of water, tending to her young. She only emerges to take audience with her enforcers and "humanoid" children.

LAMA SU

KAMINO'S PRIME MINISTER

DATA FILE

AFFILIATION: None
HOMEWORLD: Kamino
SPECIES: Kaminoan
HEIGHT: 2.29m (7ft 5in)
APPEARANCES: II
SEE ALSO: Obi-Wan Kenobi

Elongated bones allow limited flexibility in neck

Kaminoans fly on creatures called aiwhas between their cities. Aiwhas can fly and swim with equal ease.

Cloak of office

LAMA SU is Prime Minister of Kamino, where the clone army is being created. He met with Sifo-Dyas, the mysterious Jedi who placed the order for a clone army. Lama is not concerned with the use of the army, only of the financial benefit for his people.

Dexterous fingers

KAMINO IS a remote, watery planet, cut off from the larger arena of galactic events. Lama Su is only marginally interested in off-world politics, and focuses on the technical challenges of cloning a mass army.

Small feet adapted to firm Kaminoan seabed and now to hard flooring

Grand Tour

Lama Su personally takes Obi-Wan Kenobi on a tour of the cloning facility. The Prime Minister is one of the few Kaminoans to have any contact with off-worlders. But he is still not entirely comfortable in their presence. He makes no mention of Kenobi's unfamiliarity with the project.

LANAI

DATA FILE

AFFILIATION: None
HOMEWORLD: Ahch-To
SPECIES: Lanai
HEIGHT: Unknown
APPEARANCES: VIII
SEE ALSO: Luke Skywalker; Rey

Scaly skin is like shark skin rather than fish scales

THE LANAIS have lived on Temple Island for thousands of years. These humanoid creatures, who walk on two birdlike legs and have scaly fishlike heads, look after the island and its ancient Jedi buildings.

Clean white habit made from plant fibers

LANAI SOCIETY

is divided along gender lines. Females are called the "Caretakers" and they tend to the island and run life in the village. The males are fishermen called the "Visitors." They spend their lives at sea, returning to the village only once a month to celebrate the "Gathering" of fish.

In the Lanais' village, the female Caretakers follow the virtues of cleanliness, orderliness, and decorum.

Porg Neighbors

A distant relative of the Lanais, porgs are a non-sentient bird also native to Ahch-To. Both species share seabird ancestry and they exist harmoniously side by side in the rugged coastal habitat. Porgs build their nests on the cliffs of Temple Island, where they raise their young, known as porglets.

Birdlike toe arrangement

LANDO CALRISSIAN

BARON ADMINISTRATOR OF CLOUD CITY

DATA FILE

AFFILIATION: Rebel Alliance
HOMEWORLD: Unknown
SPECIES: Human
HEIGHT: 1.78m (5ft 8in)
APPEARANCES: S, V, VI
SEE ALSO: Han Solo;
L3-37; Lobot; Ugnaught

Tarelle
sel-weave shirt

Royal emblems

Lando and crew blast their way out of the Kessel spice mines with the unrefined coaxium.

DASHING LANDO CALRISSIAN

is a rogue, con artist, smuggler, and gambler, who won control of Cloud City in a game of sabacc. He has come to enjoy his newfound sense of responsibility as Baron Administrator.

LANDO'S Cloud City is a fabulous mining colony on Bespin. After leaving the city, Lando falls in with the rebels. He is promoted to general and still finds adventure, but now contributes his abilities to a greater cause.

Betrayed

Calrissian is forced to betray Han Solo and his friends to Darth Vader in order to preserve Cloud City's freedom. When he learns that the Sith Lord has no intention of keeping his side of the bargain, Lando plots a rescue mission and escapes from the city he once ruled.

In a cantina on Numidian Prime, Lando loses the *Millennium Falcon* to Han Solo during a game of sabacc.

LIEUTENANT CONNIX

COMMUNICATIONS OFFICER

DATA FILE

AFFILIATION: Resistance
HOMEWORLD: Dulathia
SPECIES: Human
HEIGHT: 1.51m (5ft 1in)
APPEARANCES: VII, VIII
SEE ALSO: Poe Dameron;
Princess Leia; PZ-4CO

KAYDEL KO CONNIX joined the Resistance as a junior operations controller in Fleet Command. After the destruction of Starkiller Base, she is promoted to lieutenant and goes on to play an instrumental role in the evacuation of D'Qar.

New lieutenant rank plaque

Brown officer uniform

COMMUNICATIONS EXPERT

Kaydel Ko Connix plays an essential role as part of the Resistance. She first proves her skill at the Battle of Starkiller Base, keeping X-wing pilots and their commanders in contact. Later, during the evacuation of D'Qar, Connix keeps everything running smoothly from the bridge of the *Raddus*.

When Princess Leia returns to duty, Connix and the other mutineers are quick to surrender to her command.

Courage of her Convictions

Connix is in on Finn and Rose Tico's secret mission to get aboard the *Supremacy* to take out the device tracking their ship, but she keeps it from Vice Admiral Holdo. She also backs Poe Dameron in his mutiny against Holdo, sealing the doors of the bridge.

LIEUTENANT MITAKA

FIRST ORDER OFFICER

DATA FILE

AFFILIATION: First Order
HOMEWORLD: Unknown
SPECIES: Human
HEIGHT: 1.8m (5ft 9in)
APPEARANCES: VII
SEE ALSO: Finn; First Order
TIE pilot; General Hux;
Kylo Ren

DOPHELD MITAKA is an attentive young officer serving aboard the First Order flagship *Finalizer*. A top graduate in his Academy class, Mitaka is not prepared for Kylo Ren's unforgiving command style.

Rank cylinders

Polished belt clasp

THE FIRST ORDER

naval uniform is descended from the sharp, authoritarian styles worn by officers of the Old Empire. The charcoal-gray fabric signifies naval service, while the flared breeches and stiff boots help in maintaining a rigid posture. The command cap carries the starburst symbol of the First Order.

Mitaka issues orders on behalf of General Hux to stop the escaping TIE fighter carrying Poe Dameron and FN-2187.

Tough Job

After failing to recapture the escaped prisoner Poe Dameron and deserter FN-2187, Mitaka continues to oversee the progress of search teams scouring the desert wastes of Jakku. Mitaka has the unenviable task of updating Kylo Ren on the search after the fugitives flee Jakku aboard the *Millennium Falcon*.

LOBOT

CLOUD CITY'S CHIEF ADMINISTRATIVE AIDE

DATA FILE

AFFILIATION: Rebel Alliance
HOMEWORLD: Bespin
SPECIES: Human cyborg
HEIGHT: 1.75m (5ft 7in)
APPEARANCES: V
SEE ALSO: Lando Calrissian

City central
computer link

Efficient and near-silent, Lobot is
the ideal assistant to flamboyant
Lando Calrissian.

Belt projects
clear-signal field

LOBOT IS CLOUD City's Chief
Administrative Aide. He keeps
in direct contact with the city's
central computer via cybernetic
implants that wrap round his
head. Lobot can monitor a
vast array of details at once.

Fineweave
sherculién-cloth shirt

THE IMPLANTS in Lobot's
brain allow him to process information at
incredible speeds, and let him retain much
of his personality. Unfortunately, during a
botched heist with Lando, Lobot had to
let the implants take complete control
of his mind, and he became, forever,
a machine-like assistant.

To the Rescue
Lobot has no special love for Palpatine's
Empire. When Lando Calrissian turns against
Darth Vader and decides to rescue Han
Solo's friends, Lobot's connection to the
central computers proves useful. In
response to Lando's "Code Force Seven,"
Lobot arrives with Cloud City guards to
free Leia, Chewbacca, and C-3PO.

LOGRAY

EWOK HEAD SHAMAN

DATA FILE

AFFILIATION: Bright Tree Village
HOMEWORLD: Forest moon of Endor
SPECIES: Ewok
HEIGHT: 1.32m (4ft 3in)
APPEARANCES: VI
SEE ALSO: Chief Chirpa

LOGRAY is an Ewok tribal shaman and medicine man. He uses his knowledge of ritual and magic to help and awe his people. The shaman still favors the old Ewok traditions of initiation and live sacrifice.

Churi skull

Logray and Chief Chirpa eventually persuade their tribe to join the rebels in their fight.

Staff of power

Striped fur

Honor Feast

Logray first decides that Han Solo, Luke Skywalker, Chewbacca, and R2-D2 will be sacrificed. They will be the main course at a banquet to honor C-3PO, who the Ewoks believe is "a golden god."

IN HIS youth, Logray was a great warrior. His staff of power is adorned with trophies, including remnants of old enemies. Logray is suspicious of all outsiders, an attitude reinforced by the arrival of Imperial forces.

LOR SAN TEKKA

WISE SURVIVALIST

DATA FILE

AFFILIATION: Church of the Force
HOMEWORLD: Unknown
SPECIES: Human
HEIGHT: 1.85m (6ft 1in)
APPEARANCES: VII
SEE ALSO: BB-8; Kylo Ren; Poe Dameron; Princess Leia

A KEEPER of obscure information, Lor San Tekka has traveled the wilds of the galaxy in pursuit of ancient relics. His secret knowledge proves vital to the survival of the Resistance.

Chain of Wisdom

Lor witnessed the early life of Kylo Ren. Enraged at Lor reminding him of simpler, more tranquil times, Kylo slays the old man.

Gundark-hide survival belt

Desperate Times

General Leia Organa is desperate to contact Lor San Tekka, believing he may have information revealing the location of her brother, the last Jedi in the galaxy. She dispatches her best pilot, Poe Dameron, to find the old traveler at Tuanul village on Jakku.

IN HIS TRAVELS

Lor San Tekka uncovered many fragments of ancient Jedi traditions that the Old Empire had worked so hard to destroy. When Luke Skywalker began researching Jedi history in the hope of restoring the Jedi Order, he learned much from Lor San Tekka.

LUKE SKYWALKER

THE LAST JEDI

DATA FILE

AFFILIATION: Jedi
HOMEWORLD: Tatooine
SPECIES: Human
HEIGHT: 1.72m (5ft 6in)
APPEARANCES: III, IV, V, VI, VII, VIII
SEE ALSO: Darth Vader; Han Solo; Princess Leia; Rey; Yoda

After years in hiding, Luke appears on Crait for one last heroic act. He gives Resistance members time to escape.

Weather shawl for Ahch-To's harsh climate

Carved walking stick

TATOOINE FARMHAND Luke Skywalker is thrown into a world of adventure when he discovers a secret message inside a new droid. Luke becomes a space pilot for the Rebel Alliance and fulfills his true destiny as a legendary Jedi Knight.

AFTER THE Empire is defeated, Luke undertakes study, travel, and spiritual contemplation, before teaching a new generation of Jedi. However, the new Jedi suffer a terrible setback with the coming of Kylo Ren. Blaming himself, Luke goes into exile and shuts himself off from the Force.

Jedi Path

Luke first climbs into the cockpit of an X-wing in the attack on the first Death Star. Fighting for the Rebel Alliance in the years afterward, Luke becomes a great leader. Yoda helps to awaken Luke's Force abilities, and, as a Jedi, Luke faces the challenges of the Emperor and Vader, holding the galaxy's hope for freedom.

LUMINARA UNDULI

MIRIALAN JEDI MASTER

DATA FILE

AFFILIATION: Jedi
HOMEWORLD: Mirial
SPECIES: Mirialan
HEIGHT: 1.7m (5ft 6in)
APPEARANCES: II, III
SEE ALSO: Barriss Offee

Traditional Mirialan headdress

Luminara Unduli is serving on Kashyyyk when she is captured by clone troopers during Order 66.

Mirialan facial tattoo

BORN ON THE COLD, dry world of Mirial, Luminara Unduli joined the Jedi Order at a young age. She fights against the droid soldiers at the Battle of Geonosis and is one of the few Jedi to survive. Unduli serves as a Jedi General in the Clone Wars.

Battle on Geonosis

Luminara Unduli and more than 200 other Jedi fight Count Dooku's army in the Geonosis arena. When Jedi Master Yoda arrives with the newly created clone army, Unduli quickly takes command of a unit of soldiers to wage war in a great land battle against the Separatists.

LUMINARA UNDULI dies in an Imperial prison on Stygeon Prime. The Grand Inquisitor uses rumors of her survival and the lingering Force presence of her remains to draw out Jedi survivors.

LYN ME

PERFORMER IN THE MAX REBO BAND

DATA FILE

AFFILIATION: Jabba's court
HOMEWORLD: Ryloth
SPECIES: Twi'lek
HEIGHT: 1.6m (5ft 3in)
APPEARANCES: VI
SEE ALSO: Greeata; Rystáll

Sensua bindings

Elegant hand position

Lyn Me travels the galaxy with the Max Rebo Band.

Lekku (head-tail)

LYN ME IS A TWI'LEK dancer and backup singer in the Max Rebo Band at Jabba's palace. She studied Twi'lek dance and quickly gained the attention of Max Rebo, who is constantly on the lookout for new talent.

LYN ME grew up on the barren northern continent of Ryloth, the Twi'leks' homeworld. Her species has suffered generations of hardships, with many Twi'leks being sold into slavery by the criminal underworld that exists in their culture.

Dance shoes

Rescued

Boba Fett saved the young Lyn Me and many others from slavery. Her village elders had pooled their meager resources to pay the famed bounty hunter to exterminate the slavers. As a result, Lyn Me hero-worships Fett. While dancing at Jabba's palace, she spots Boba Fett, and makes plans to talk to him.

LYRA ERSO

JYN ERSO'S MOTHER

DATA FILE

AFFILIATION: None
HOMEWORLD: Aria Prime
SPECIES: Human
HEIGHT: 1.7m (5ft 6in)
APPEARANCES: RO
SEE ALSO: Galen Erso;
Jyn Erso; Orson Krennic

LYRA ERSO IS the wife of the eminent crystallographer Galen Erso and the mother of Jyn Erso. She and Galen met through work, but his research spells the end of her career and ultimately the whole family's downfall.

Robes made from homespun sativa plant fibers

Lyra gives her daughter, Jyn, a fragment of a kyber crystal on a necklace as a good omen.

Red is the color of the Force-attuned sect the Enlightened

Tracked down

When it becomes clear that the Empire has its sights on Galen's research, Lyra and Galen flee with their young daughter, Jyn. After four years the Empire catches up with them. Jyn escapes, as she has been trained to, Galen is taken away, and Lyra does not survive the encounter.

Comlink for contacting family in an emergency

INQUISITIVE and intelligent, Lyra studies the history and philosophy of the Jedi Order. She also helps Galen with his research, though she is the first to become suspicious of his colleague Orson Krennic.

MACE WINDU

LEGENDARY JEDI MASTER

DATA FILE

AFFILIATION: Jedi
HOMEWORLD: Haruun Kal
SPECIES: Human
HEIGHT: 1.88m (6ft 2in)
APPEARANCES: I, II, III
SEE ALSO: Anakin
Skywalker; Palpatine; Yoda

A master of combat, Mace Windu is one of the best living lightsaber fighters.

MACE WINDU IS a senior member of the Jedi High Council. His wisdom and combat prowess are legendary. Windu is somber and cool-minded, but he is also capable of dramatic actions in the face of danger.

Jedi utility belt

Coarseweave tunic

Gut Instinct

Mace Windu's suspicions about Chancellor Palpatine are proven right when Anakin reveals that Palpatine is a Sith Lord. Windu takes immediate action, promising to take Palpatine into Jedi custody dead or alive.

MACE IS decisive and perceptive. He is one of the first Jedi to sense danger in Anakin Skywalker and is quick to lead a Jedi taskforce to Geonosis when war preparations are discovered there.

Tunic allows ease of movement in combat

Boots offer excellent traction

During Mace's duel with Darth Sidious, Anakin has to choose whether to betray his teachings or help capture the Sith Lord.

MAGNAGUARD

GENERAL GRIEVOUS' DROID BODYGUARDS

DATA FILE

AFFILIATION: Separatists
TYPE: Bodyguard droid
MANUFACTURER: Holowan Mechanicals
HEIGHT: 1.95m (6ft 4in)
APPEARANCES: III
SEE ALSO: General Grievous

Primary photoreceptors

GENERAL GRIEVOUS' bodyguards are built to the alien cyborg's own specifications and trained by him. MagnaGuards often fight in pairs and can adjust their combat styles to match those of their opponents. They are equipped with deadly electrostaffs, or grenades and rocket launchers.

Mumuu cloak markings match those on Grievous' mask

Electrostaffs are resistant to lightsaber strikes

Cloak is combat-tattered

MAGNAGUARDS

replicate the elite group of warriors and bodyguards that would always accompany Grievous when he was a Kaleesh warlord. Other Separatist leaders, including Count Dooku, come to use the MagnaGuards as bodyguards or soldiers.

Battle-scarred legs

MagnaGuards use their electrostaffs to stun or kill opponents.

Double Trouble

Anakin Skywalker and Obi-Wan Kenobi fight two MagnaGuards, IG-101 and IG-102, on Grievous' command ship *Invisible Hand*, when they attempt to rescue Palpatine. Even when Kenobi slices the head off one of the droids, it uses backup processors to continue fighting!

MAJOR BRANCE

COMMAND CENTER OFFICER

DATA FILE

AFFILIATION: Resistance
HOMEWORLD: Rinn
SPECIES: Human
HEIGHT: 1.75m (5ft 7in)
APPEARANCES: VII
SEE ALSO: Admiral Statura;
C-3PO; General Ematt;
Princess Leia

A COMMUNICATIONS officer based in the Resistance command center on D'Qar, Major Taslin Brance keeps the upper ranks informed of the changing fortunes of the Resistance, and the growing threat of the First Order.

Major rank badge, army service

Resistance operations tunic

WITH FEW resources, the Resistance relies on up-to-the-minute intelligence in order to best prioritize missions against the First Order. Dispatchers and comm officers like Brance monitor transmissions from across the galaxy, seeking patterns, clues, and signs of danger.

Bad News

During the search for Luke Skywalker, Brance grows weary of always passing bad news to General Leia Organa. It is Brance who updates Organa with news that Lor San Tekka has been killed, and that Poe Dameron is missing and believed dead in the same First Order raid. He also reports on the first firing of the massive Starkiller weapon.

Brance knows that poor intelligence can cost lives, and works hard to avoid mistakes.

MALAKILI

KEEPER OF JABBA'S RANCOR

DATA FILE

AFFILIATION: Jabba's court
HOMEWORLD: Corellia
SPECIES: Human
HEIGHT: 1.72m (5ft 6in)
APPEARANCES: VI
SEE ALSO: Jabba the Hutt

JABBA'S CHIEF ANIMAL HANDLER, Malakili, looks after a murderous rancor that Jabba keeps beneath his throne room. Jabba loves throwing anyone who displeases him into the rancor's den, and Malakili tends any wounds that the monster receives from its unwilling snacks.

Sweat-soaked rag belt

Wrist guard

Ancient circus pants

MALAKILI once worked as an animal handler in a traveling circus. When one of his dangerous beasts escaped during a show on Nar Shaddaa and killed audience members, Malakili was enslaved. After this incident, Malakili was sold to Jabba the Hutt.

Jabba's rancor once saved Malakili's life when Sand People attacked him.

Beloved Pet

Both Malakili and his fellow animal handler, Giran, are very fond of the rancor that they care for. It is their favorite animal in Jabba's palace. Luke Skywalker slays the brutal beast after it attempts to devour him, and Malakili and Giran weep openly.

MAS AMEDDA

CHAGRIAN SENATE SPEAKER

DATA FILE

AFFILIATION: Republic/Empire
HOMEWORLD: Champala
SPECIES: Chagrian
HEIGHT: 1.96m (6ft 4in)
APPEARANCES: I, II, III
SEE ALSO: Palpatine

Attack and display horns

Speaker's staff

MAS AMEDDA IS SPEAKER of the Galactic Senate on Coruscant where he keeps order in debates. Amedda is a stern and stoic Chagrian, and is one of a select few who understand that Palpatine is more than he appears to be.

Blue skin screens out harmful radiation

Robes of state

Amedda is the first to suggest that the Senate should give Palpatine emergency powers.

DURING Valorum's term as Supreme Chancellor, Mas Amedda is Vice Chair of the Galactic Senate. Secretly working for Palpatine, Amedda does everything in his power to tie up the Senate in endless debates so that Valorum loses the support of many senators.

Standing Firm

Mas Amedda is by Palpatine's side after the fight with Yoda in the Senate, when Palpatine's personal shock troopers search for signs of the Jedi Master. After Palpatine transforms the Republic into the Galactic Empire, Amedda serves as his Grand Vizier.

MAUL

SITH SURVIVOR AND CRIME LORD

DATA FILE

AFFILIATION: Sith, Nightbrothers, Crimson Dawn
HOMEWORLD: Dathomir
SPECIES: Zabrak
HEIGHT: 1.75m (5ft 7in)
APPEARANCES: I, S
SEE ALSO: Qi'ra; Qui-Gon Jinn; Obi-Wan Kenobi

Field cloak

Lightsaber blade is red due to nature of internal crystals

YEARS AGO, Maul served as Darth Sidious' apprentice as one of the most dangerous and highly trained Sith in the history of the Order. To honor his heritage as part of the warrior clan known as the Nightbrothers of Dathmir, he had his entire body marked with tribal patterns.

MAUL WAS believed dead by the Jedi, but his lust for vengeance kept him alive. Reanimated by Nightsister magicks, Maul returned during the Clone Wars to wreak havoc in the criminal underworld before being captured by Darth Sidious. Maul once again narrowly escaped death.

Maul Versus Kenobi

Sent to capture Queen Amidala, Maul gives Qui-Gon Jinn and Obi-Wan Kenobi the rare opportunity to fight a trained Sith warrior. Jinn first duels with Maul on Tatooine. He later faces Maul on Naboo, this time with Kenobi. Kenobi thought he had destroyed the evil Sith, but Maul survived the devastating wound.

During the time of the Galactic Empire, Maul leads the ruthless crime syndicate Crimson Dawn.

MAX REBO

LEADER OF JABBA'S HOUSE BAND

THE BLUE ORTOLAN, known in the entertainment business as Max Rebo, is a half-insane keyboard player who is completely obsessed with food. When the pleasure-loving crime boss Jabba the Hutt offers Max a contract that pays only in free meals, he immediately accepts—to the outrage of his bandmates!

Signed

Jabba is so enthusiastic about the wild music that the Max Rebo Band plays, he offers the band a lifetime gig at his palace. The band is playing when Luke Skywalker enters the palace to try to free Han Solo. After Jabba's death, the band breaks up.

Output speaker

Ears store fat

Air intake

Articulated toes can absorb food and drink

FOR AN

Ortolan, Max Rebo is quite skinny. His obsession with food may lead him to have poor judgment as the leader of his band, but he is devoted to music and quite good at his chosen instrument— the red ball jet organ.

Max Rebo's band accompanies Jabba's entourage on the Hutt's sail barge.

MAZ KANATA

DATA FILE

AFFILIATION: Pirate
HOMEWORLD: Takodana
SPECIES: Unknown
HEIGHT: 1.24m (4ft 1in)
APPEARANCES: VII, VIII
SEE ALSO: Finn; Han Solo;
Princess Leia; Rey

Variable lens
corrective goggles

Bracelet of
the Sutro

Clothes knitted
by Maz herself

A MISCHIEVOUS PIRATE
boss who has spent
centuries surviving in the
galaxy's fringe, Maz is
regarded with respect
by some of the toughest
gangsters in space. Maz
has a strong connection
to the Force, but she
is no Jedi.

MAZ'S HOSPITALITY is

legendary, and she invites
independent starship crews
to visit her castle keep on
Takodana. As long as
guests don't cause trouble,
and grudges and politics
are left at the door, Maz is
happy to host all manner of
law-bending wanderers in her home.

Scoundrel's Reunion

Han Solo has known Maz Kanata for decades,
and describes her as an "acquired taste."
Though she is small, Maz has a big and playful
personality, passing on her wisdom with
equal parts good humor and stinging
criticism. Solo visits Maz after an absence of
25 years, to get help finding the Resistance.
As Solo brings with him two fugitives from
the First Order, evil forces close in and the
Resistance soon comes to him.

ME-8D9

ANCIENT PROTOCOL DROID

DATA FILE

AFFILIATION: None
HOMEWORLD: Takodana
MANUFACTURER: Unknown
HEIGHT: 1.72m (5ft 6in)
APPEARANCES: VII
SEE ALSO: Bazine Netal;
Maz Kanata

KNOWN AS "Emmie" to the scoundrels within Maz's castle on Takodana, ME-8D9 is a protocol droid who is often called on to translate the less-than-legal deals made within the castle's dining and gaming halls.

Shielded data
storage center

Bronzium-enriched finish

EMMIE IS an ancient droid of an unknown model, and rumor has it that she is as old as the castle itself. Emmie has little memory of her original functions, and she has been reprogrammed countless times.

Knee assembly

Reinforced ankle joint

Mysterious Past

Fragments of Emmie's past surface occasionally—a side effect of her outdated design. Though mainly built for protocol duty, she has also served as an assassin for shady criminals, including the notorious Crymorah. There are some who believe she was originally in the service of the ancient Jedi Order.

MOFF JERJERROD

SUPERVISOR OF THE SECOND DEATH STAR

DATA FILE

AFFILIATION: Empire
HOMEWORLD: Tinnel IV
SPECIES: Human
HEIGHT: 1.83m (6ft)
APPEARANCES: VI
SEE ALSO: Captain Needa;
Darth Vader

MOFF JERJERROD SUPERVISES the construction of the second Death Star. During the Battle of Endor, Jerjerrod commands the station's superlaser against the rebel forces. He is killed when the rebels finally detonate the Death Star's reactor.

Imperial code cylinder

Rank insignia plaque

Imperial officer's tunic

Jerjerrod blames slow progress of the Death Star's construction on a shortfall of workers.

Naval boots

JERJERROD was born to a wealthy family on the Core World of Tinnel IV. He shows petty spitefulness and a lack of ambition as he rises through the Imperial ranks—both admirable qualities in a Moff. When he is assigned to the top secret second Death Star project, his cover title is Director of Imperial Energy Systems.

Called to Account

When the construction of the Death Star falls behind schedule, the Emperor sends Vader to put additional pressure on Moff Jerjerrod and his construction crews. Informed that the Emperor himself will soon be arriving, Jerjerrod assures Vader his men will double their efforts.

MOLOCH

WHITE WORMS ENFORCER

DATA FILE

AFFILIATION: White Worms
HOMEWORLD: Corellia
SPECIES: Grindalid
HEIGHT: 2m (6ft 6in)
APPEARANCES: S
SEE ALSO: Han Solo; Lady Proxima; Qi'ra

Mask protects skin from sunlight

A BRUTISH Grindalid named Moloch is an enforcer for Lady Proxima and her gang, the White Worms. The Grindalids run the black market in Coronet City and eat a diet of rats brought to them by their network of underlings.

Scepter decorated with writhing scrumrats

Resourceful scrumrats who prove to be useful can be promoted to engage in more serious crime.

Salt-encrusted clothes from wet, briny throne room

MOST GRINDALIDS

stay hidden away in their den because Corellia's sun burns their skin, but Moloch ventures outside. He wears long clothes and a mask so every part of his body is covered. He has also trained himself to move on his tail as though he has human legs.

Loyal Servant

Moloch serves his "dear matriarch," Lady Proxima. She leads the criminal gang that runs a horde of human "scrumrats": desperate children forced to catch rats for her hatchlings, pick pockets, and commit other petty crimes. Han Solo and Qi'ra began their criminal careers as scrumrats.

MON MOTHMA

REBEL ALLIANCE LEADER

DATA FILE

AFFILIATION: Republic/Rebel Alliance/New Republic
HOMEWORLD: Chandrila
SPECIES: Human
HEIGHT: 1.73m (5ft 7in)
APPEARANCES: III, RO, VI
SEE ALSO: Bail Organa

Simple Chandrilan hairstyle

MON MOTHMA IS THE highest leader of the Rebellion. As a member of the Galactic Senate, she champions the cause of freedom until the Emperor's evil closes in around her. Abandoning the Senate, Mothma works with Bail Organa to form the Rebel Alliance that aims to unseat the Galactic Empire.

Hanna pendant

Elegant robe of Fleuréline weave

Gesture of reconciliation

Mon Mothma listens to all the opinions on the Rebel Council about the alleged Death Star.

Shraa silk mantle

MON MOTHMA was born into a political family and became the youngest senator to enter the Senate. When the Republic collapses, she goes underground and begins to organize the various cells of resistance into a single entity: The Alliance to Restore the Republic (or Rebel Alliance).

Rebel Founders

Mon Mothma and Bail Organa become convinced that Palpatine needs to be opposed. With the Senate under Palpatine's control, and his newly appointed governors overseeing all star systems, the two loyalists make a pact with a few dependable Senators to form a highly secret Rebellion movement.

MUDTROOPER

IMPERIAL SWAMP TROOPERS

DATA FILE

AFFILIATION: Empire
HOMEWORLD: Various
STANDARD EQUIPMENT:
E-10 blaster rifle
APPEARANCES: S
SEE ALSO: Han Solo;
Tobias Beckett

THE IMPERIAL ARMY relies on regular troops alongside its stormtroopers. On the swampy planet of Mimban, mudtroopers of the 244th Imperial Armored Division are caught in a quagmire, fighting local Mimbanese guerillas.

Respirator mask for hazardous air

Waterproof capes nicknamed "slicks"

Han is sent to Mimban after being expelled from the Imperial pilot academy.

Camp Forward

Conditions on misty, swampy Mimban are harsh. Aside from the local insurgency threat, there is the risk of trench foot from the marshy ground and lung disease from fungal spores in the air. Mudtroopers cannot even drink vaporated water because it contains harmful microbes.

FEW CHOOSE the life of a mudtrooper. Most of the soldiers on Mimban were conscripted. However, some were sent as punishment for insubordination in other parts of the army, and a few agreed to serve there in exchange for a military scholarship.

NABOO GUARD

BODYGUARD OF THE NABOO MONARCHY

DATA FILE

AFFILIATION: Royal Naboo Security Forces
HOMEWORLD: Naboo
SPECIES: Human
APPEARANCES: I, II
SEE ALSO: Captain Panaka

THE NABOO ROYAL GUARD is the highly trained bodyguard of the Naboo monarch and court. Its loyal, dedicated soldiers typically experience battle off-planet and return to Naboo to protect the royal house out of loyalty.

Naboo forces use small Gian landspeeders in their attempt to repel the invading droid army.

Blast-damping armor

Unarmored joints for agility

Utility belt

No leg armor for mobility

THE ROYAL GUARD

forms one component of the Naboo Royal Security Forces. Its members work alongside the Security Guard, which comprises mainly sentries and patrolmen, and the Space Fighter Corps, which flies N-1 starfighters.

Shin protectors

Returning Forces

When the Trade Federation droid army invades Naboo, the Royal Guard gets its first taste of true battle. But the sheer number of battle droids means a defeat for Naboo. Fortunately, Queen Amidala and the Head of Security, Captain Panaka, escape and are able to return, with the Gungans, to put an end to the droid occupation.

NIEN NUNB

HEROIC SULLUSTAN PILOT

DATA FILE

AFFILIATION: Rebel Alliance/
Resistance
HOMEWORLD: Sullust
SPECIES: Sullustan
HEIGHT: 1.79m (5ft 9in)
APPEARANCES: VI, VII, VIII
SEE ALSO: Lando Calrissian;
Poe Dameron; Princess Leia

NIEN NUNB is Lando Calrissian's
Sullustan copilot on board the
Millennium Falcon at the Battle
of Endor. Lando understands
the Sullustan language that
Nunb speaks, and personally
picks him for the mission,
impressed by Nunb's exploits
aboard his own renowned
vessel, the *Mellcrawler*.

Tool pouch

Pressurized g-suit

Flight gauntlets

Gear harness

NIEN NUNB is one of many
Sullustans who serve as fighter pilots
in the Rebel Alliance. His homeworld,
Sullust, is the staging area for the
rebel fleet before the Battle of Endor.
The Alliance award Nunb a medal
named the Kalidor Crescent for his
bravery in the battle.

Nunb serves in the depleted
Resistance fleet under Vice
Admiral Holdo. He survives
D'Qar and then Crait.

Positive-grip boots

Trusted Pilot

Nunb learned his piloting skills flying a freighter
for the Sullustan SoroSuub Corporation. When
SoroSuub begins to support the Empire, Nunb
shows his opposition by stealing from the
company on behalf of the Rebel Alliance.
At first, Nunb works as an independent
smuggler, but he eventually becomes
a full-time member of the Alliance.

NUTE GUNRAY

NEIMOIDIAN VICEROY

DATA FILE

AFFILIATION: Trade Federation, Separatists
HOMEWORLD: Neimoidia
SPECIES: Neimoidian
HEIGHT: 1.91m (6ft 3in)
APPEARANCES: I, II, III
SEE ALSO: Padmé Amidala; Palpatine

Viceroy's crested tiara

THE VICEROY OF THE Trade Federation, Nute Gunray, is powerful, deceitful, and willing to kill for his far-reaching commercial aims. Gunray becomes an unwitting pawn of Darth Sidious when he agrees to invade the peaceful planet of Naboo.

Wheedling expression

The Trade Federation secretly aids the Separatists during the Clone Wars.

Viceroy's collar

Sidious will need the Trade Federation's help only until his control of the galaxy is assured.

NUTE GUNRAY

is a Neimoidian, a species known for its exceptional greed. Gunray makes an alliance with Darth Sidious to blockade Naboo in opposition to increased taxation. However, Gunray feels increasingly uneasy when his alliance with Sidious leads to open warfare.

True Face

Gunray's true cowardice shows itself when Padmé Amidala's freedom fighters storm the Royal Palace. Unable to hide behind battle droids any longer, Gunray is arrested. It is a sign of the Republic's decay that he is later able to buy his release and continue as Viceroy of the Trade Federation.

OBI-WAN KENOBI

LEGENDARY JEDI MASTER

DATA FILE

AFFILIATION: Jedi
HOMEWORLD: Stewjon
SPECIES: Human
HEIGHT: 1.79m (5ft 9in)
APPEARANCES: I, II, III, IV, V, VI
SEE ALSO: Anakin Skywalker; Luke Skywalker

Under-tunic

Jedi robe

Kenobi faces Darth Vader—known previously as his Padawan, Anakin Skywalker—in battle.

OBI-WAN KENOBI is a truly great Jedi who finds himself at the heart of galactic turmoil as the Republic unravels and finally collapses. Although cautious by nature, Kenobi has a healthy independent streak and truly formidable lightsaber skills.

KENOBI'S path is destined to lead in a very different direction to that of his Jedi partner, Anakin Skywalker. After Order 66, Kenobi helps protect Luke Skywalker and Leia Organa. For many years, he hides on Tatooine, watching over young Luke, the last hope for the ancient Jedi Order.

Kenobi's considered approach to situations often conflicts with Anakin's brash nature.

General Kenobi

Kenobi becomes a great Jedi General and pilot in the Clone Wars (despite his reluctance to flying). Trained by the headstrong Qui-Gon Jinn, Kenobi trains his own master's protégé, Anakin Skywalker, after Jinn's death. The bond between Kenobi and Anakin is strong as they fight through the Clone Wars.

OOLA

TWI'LEK DANCER

DATA FILE

AFFILIATION: Jabba's court
HOMEWORLD: Ryloth
SPECIES: Twi'lek
HEIGHT: 1.6m (5ft 3in)
APPEARANCES: VI
SEE ALSO: Jabba the Hutt

OOLA IS A green-skinned Twi'lek dancer enslaved to the cruel crime lord Jabba the Hutt. Jabba's majordomo, Bib Fortuna, kidnapped Oola from a primitive clan. He had other Twi'lek girls train Oola in the art of exotic dancing, so he could present her to his boss.

Lekku (head-tail)

Leather straps

Oola dances for her life in Jabba's palace, but ends up in the dreaded rancor pit.

Flimsy net costume

OOLA'S LIFE is tragic and short. Enslaved by Bib Fortuna, a stranger offers her the chance to escape in Mos Eisley. However, Fortuna has fed her so many lies about the glory of Jabba's palace that she wants to see it for herself, so she refuses this opportunity to be free.

Gruesome End

Jabba lavishes particular attention on Oola, keeping her chained to his throne. However, when Oola once more refuses Jabba's advances, the revolting Hutt is infuriated. He opens the trap door beneath the dance floor and watches as Oola is fed to his deadly rancor monster.

OPPO RANCISIS

JEDI HIGH COUNCIL MEMBER

DATA FILE

AFFILIATION: Jedi
HOMEWORLD: Thisspias
SPECIES: Thisspiasian
HEIGHT: 1.38m (4ft 5in)
APPEARANCES: I, II
SEE ALSO: Yaddle

OPPO RANCISIS IS a Thisspiasian Jedi Master who sits on the Jedi High Council. He joined the Jedi Order as an infant, and trained under Master Yaddle. When offered the throne of Thisspias, he declined it to continue to serve the galaxy as a Jedi. He is now a top Jedi military advisor.

Dense hair deters biting cygnats of Thisspias

RANCISIS is an excellent strategist, who ensures that, if negotiation fails, Jedi-counseled military tactics are cunning and effective. During the Clone Wars, Rancisis fights in the Siege of Saleucami, but also spends much time on Coruscant, coordinating Republic forces throughout the galaxy.

Master Jedi

Rancisis is adept with his green-bladed lightsaber, but prefers to use his highly developed Force powers for combat. He is a formidable foe in unarmed combat, using his four arms and long tail to make surprising strikes at his opponent.

Second pair of hands hidden underneath cloak

Fingers tipped with claws

ORSON KRENNIC

DIRECTOR OF WEAPONS RESEARCH

ORSON KRENNIC

DATA FILE

AFFILIATION: Empire
HOMEWORLD: Lexrul
SPECIES: Human
HEIGHT: 1.8m (5ft 9in)
APPEARANCES: RO
SEE ALSO: Galen Erso; Grand Moff Tarkin; Supreme Leader Snoke

A DIRECTOR of the Empire's Advanced Weapons Research Division, Orson Krennic heads up the Tarkin Initiative—the think tank responsible for creating the Death Star. He reached this exalted position thanks to his scientific mind and ruthless ambition.

Rank plaque shows the equivalent of Admiral

Coded key cylinder

DT-29 heavy blaster pistol

KRENNIC'S thirst for power knows no bounds, but working for the Imperial leadership is precarious. Even after a successful test shot on Jedha, Orson is grateful to leave his encounter with Darth Vader with his job and his life.

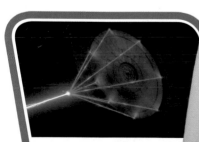

On seeing the awe-inspiring capacity of kyber crystals, Krennic's first thought is to weaponize them.

Science at any Cost

Krennic sees the devastating potential in Galen Erso's research while they are science colleagues. When Erso does not share Krennic's vision, the cruel Imperial agent has no qualms about capturing Erso, destroying his family, and forcing him to work under duress.

OWEN LARS

LUKE SKYWALKER'S GUARDIAN

DATA FILE

AFFILIATION: None
HOMEWORLD: Tatooine
SPECIES: Human
HEIGHT: 1.7m (5ft 6in)
APPEARANCES: II, III, IV
SEE ALSO: Beru Lars; Cliegg Lars; Luke Skywalker

AS A YOUNG NEWLYWED, Owen Lars made a huge decision. He agreed to hide and protect a baby from the wrath of his own father: Darth Vader. The baby was named Luke by his mother, Padmé, moments before she died in childbirth. Owen gained a nephew, but also added to his worries.

Rough clothing made in Anchorhead

Simple overcoat provides warmth in the cold desert evenings

Tool pouch

YOUNG OWEN was born to Cliegg Lars and his first wife, Aika. He has spent most of his life on his father's homestead on Tatooine, which he inherited after Cliegg passed away. Owen falls in love with Beru after meeting her in nearby Anchorhead. It is Beru who convinces the reluctant Owen to adopt Anakin's son.

Owen, his wife, Beru, and father Cliegg met Luke's parents, Anakin and Padmé, only once.

A Farmer's Life

When Luke has grown up, he works closely with Owen on the family homestead. They maintain the vaporators that collect precious moisture from the desert air, and buy "used" droids from passing Jawas. Although the teenage Luke is ready to fly the nest, Owen finds it hard to shrug off the gruff, protective attitude that has become a habit over the years.

PADMÉ AMIDALA

NABOO QUEEN AND SENATOR

DATA FILE

AFFILIATION: Royal House of Naboo, Galactic Senate
HOMEWORLD: Naboo
SPECIES: Human
HEIGHT: 1.65m (5ft 4in)
APPEARANCES: I, II, III
SEE ALSO: Anakin Skywalker; Captain Panaka

Hair pulled tightly back for clear view of enemy

Slashes in clothing sustained in Geonosian arena battle

PADMÉ GREW

up in a small Naboo village. Exceptionally talented, she was elected queen at the age of only 14. At the end of her term of office, Padmé is made senator of Naboo. It is on the Galactic capital, Coruscant, that she becomes closer to Anakin Skywalker.

PADMÉ AMIDALA HAS TIME and again found herself at the center of galactic events. From the invasion of her home planet, Naboo, to a death sentence in a Geonosian arena, by way of multiple attempts on her life as a senator, Padmé faces extraordinary danger with determination and great bravery.

Light shin armor

Action boots with firm grip

Padmé and Anakin surrender to the love they share, though they know it breaks Jedi rules.

Queen Turned Fighter

As the young Queen of Naboo, Padmé Amidala has to learn that her cherished values of nonviolence will not save her people from a brutal droid invasion. Discarding her formal robes of state, Padmé determines to inspire her own troops to end the invasion by capturing the Neimoidian leaders.

PAIGE TICO

RESISTANCE BOMBER

DATA FILE

AFFILIATION: Resistance
HOMEWORLD: Hays Minor
SPECIES: Human
HEIGHT: Unknown
APPEARANCES: VIII
SEE ALSO: Rose Tico;
Tallie Lintra

Tight-fitting
flight cap

PAIGE TICO and her sister Rose have always done everything together, including joining the Resistance. They hope to see the galaxy one day, but for now Paige is a Resistance pilot, with many successful missions under her belt.

Buoyancy
foam-filled
flight vest collar

Atmosphere hose

AS THE VENTRAL

gunner, Paige usually flies in a rotating ball turret under the bomb racks, firing repeating laser cannons. Pilots can be very superstitious and Paige is no exception. She sometimes wraps her medallion around the struts of her cannons.

Paige flies in the *Cobalt Hammer*, an MG-100 StarFortress bomber, in the Cobalt Squadron.

Resistance Hero

At D'Qar, the Resistance has the rare chance to take out a First Order Dreadnought, but all hope seems lost when no one can trigger the bombs. With all her might, Paige manages to release the 1,048 proton bombs. She cannot save herself, but the *Fulminatrix*'s destruction enables the rest of the Resistance to escape.

PALPATINE

SITH LORD AND GALACTIC EMPEROR

DATA FILE

AFFILIATION: Sith, Republic, Empire
HOMEWORLD: Naboo
SPECIES: Human
HEIGHT: 1.78m (5ft 8in)
APPEARANCES: I, II, III, V, VI
SEE ALSO: Darth Vader

Hood to hide face

PALPATINE is known by many names. Born on Naboo, Sheev Palpatine becomes his homeworld's senator. Then, he is Supreme Chancellor Palpatine. Finally, he declares himself Emperor and rules the galaxy. Ultimate power has been his plan all along. Palpatine is secretly Darth Sidious, the most evil of Sith Lords.

Palpatine secretly plans the Clone Wars to destroy the Galactic Republic and the Jedi Order.

PALPATINE

manages to keep all those around him from suspecting his true identity. For years, he has appeared patient and unassuming, so few have recognized his political ambitions. His dark side powers even blinded the Jedi from seeing behind his mask of affability.

Sensing Vader's defeat on Mustafar, Palpatine travels to his apprentice's side.

Sith Powers

His face twisted and scarred by the dark energies of the Force, Emperor Palpatine is a figure of terrible power. One of his most deadly weapons is Sith lightning, which is projected from his fingertips. A Force user can block the lethal energy for a while if they are strong, but it takes immense effort.

PAO

FIERCE REBEL COMMANDO

DATA FILE

AFFILIATION: Rebel Alliance
HOMEWORLD: Pipada
SPECIES: Drabatan
HEIGHT: 1.72m (5ft 6in)
APPEARANCES: RO
SEE ALSO:
Bistan

Antenna on backpack

PAO IS A soldier with the Rebel Alliance Special Forces. In battle, you hear him coming before you see him. Drabatans have booming voices, and Pao puts his to good use with a blood-chilling war cry.

Black-market blaster

External tibanna gas chamber

PAO IS AN

explosives expert who has also studied structural engineering. He specializes in demolitions, particularly underwater. As an amphibian, he can thrive on both land and in the water, though he prefers freshwater to the salty seawater of Scarif.

Pao's thirst for battle is exceeded only by his hatred of the Empire.

Water-shedding fatigues

Fearless Fighter

Pao is quick to volunteer for the rogue mission to Scarif as part of the historic team who retrieve the Death Star plans. While Jyn Erso and Cassian Andor sneak into the Citadel Tower, Pao and his squad are tasked with causing a distraction on the ground and making ten soldiers look like 100.

PATROL TROOPER

CORONET CITY POLICE

Enlarged helmets have improved visual displays

DATA FILE

AFFILIATION: Empire
SPECIES: Human
STANDARD VEHICLE: C-PH patrol speeder bike
STANDARD EQUIPMENT: EC-17 hold-out blasters
APPEARANCES: RO
SEE ALSO: Stormtrooper

AS THE EMPIRE tightens its grip on new worlds, it replaces local defense forces with its own specialist military law enforcement agencies. Patrol troopers are the Imperial answer to stormtrooper city policing.

Fabric gives legs more flexibility than armor

A patrol trooper fails to catch Han Solo and Qi'ra, who are speeding through Coronet City.

PATROL TROOPERS

are the urban equivalent of scout troopers, who are deployed in wilderness areas like the moon of Endor. They cruise city streets ensuring law and order. Like scout troopers, they wear protective helmets and chest armor, but stop short of full stormtrooper armor.

City Speeders

On Corellia, patrol troopers ride C-PH patrol speeder bikes. These chunky, single-rider bikes are small enough to maneuver in tight spots, but also robust in a collision. Patrol troopers receive real-time highway intel to avoid the worst traffic.

PLO KOON

JEDI HIGH COUNCIL MEMBER

DATA FILE

AFFILIATION: Jedi
HOMEWORLD: Dorin
SPECIES: Kel Dor
HEIGHT: 1.88m (6ft 2in)
APPEARANCES: I, II, III
SEE ALSO: Ki-Adi-Mundi;
Qui-Gon Jinn

Antiox mask

Plo Koon's starfighter crashes into a city on the Neimoidian planet of Cato Neimoidia.

Thick hide covers body

Loose Jedi cloak

PLO KOON is a member of the Jedi High Council and a Jedi General in the Clone Wars. He is one of the most powerful Jedi ever, with awesome fighting abilities and strong telekinetic powers. He also discovered Ahsoka Tano as an infant and inducted her into the Jedi Order.

PLO KOON

is a Kel Dor from Dorin. He wears a special mask to protect his sensitive eyes and nostrils from the oxygen-rich atmosphere of planets such as Coruscant. Master Koon fights in the Battle of Geonosis and many more conflicts in the Clone Wars.

Tragic Mission

At the end of the Clone Wars, Plo Koon, an expert pilot, leads a starfighter patrol above Cato Neimoidia. Without warning, his own clone troopers begin firing at his ship. Order 66 had been given, causing all the pre-programmed clones to turn on their Jedi leaders. Koon's ship crashes into the planet, and he is killed.

Practical combat/flight boots

POE DAMERON

BEST PILOT IN THE GALAXY

Poe's astromech droid, BB-8, serves him well.

AN INCREDIBLY skilled starfighter pilot, Poe Dameron is a commander in the Resistance's fight against the First Order. He soars into battle as Black Leader, behind the controls of a specially modified T-70 X-wing.

Insulated flight suit

POE GREW UP hearing legends of the fighter pilots of the Rebel Alliance from his mother, Shara Bey, who flew an A-wing during the Battle of Endor. Poe's father was Kes Dameron, a Rebel Alliance Pathfinder soldier.

Glie-44 blaster

Rebellious Rebel

Poe displays his fearless flying over D'Qar. In a single, lightweight starfighter, he gets right up to the First Order dreadnought the *Fulminatrix* and takes out its surface cannons. Then he is reckless. Disobeying orders to disengage, he continues to lead the charge to bring down the ship, but at the cost of the Resistance's whole bomber fleet.

155

POGGLE THE LESSER

GEONOSIAN ARCHDUKE

DATA FILE

AFFILIATION: Separatists
HOMEWORLD: Geonosis
SPECIES: Geonosian
HEIGHT: 1.83m (6ft)
APPEARANCES: II, III
SEE ALSO:
Count Dooku;
Geonosian
soldier

THE ARCHDUKE OF GEONOSIS,
Poggle the Lesser, rules the
Stalgasin hive colony, which controls
all the other major hive colonies
on Geonosis. His factories build
innumerable battle droids for the
Separatists, using the labor of
legions of downtrodden drones.

Long wattles

POGGLE emerged from
a lower caste through the sheer
force of his iron will to become
Archduke. He is the public face
of the Geonosian aristocracy
and arms business. Hidden
beneath the hives of his planet
is his monarch, Karina the Great,
an enormous Geonosian queen
whose vast egg chambers
propagate the species.

High-caste
wings

Aristocratic
adornments

Command
staff

Commissioned to design a
superweapon, Poggle hands
the plans to Count Dooku.

Presiding Leaders

Poggle the Lesser presides over
the first meeting of the Separatist
leadership on his planet, as well
as the trial of Anakin Skywalker,
Obi-Wan Kenobi, and Padmé
Amidala, who are accused of spying.
Poggle and the other Separatists
take refuge in the underlevels
when Republic forces arrive.

PONDA BABA

DATA FILE

AFFILIATION: Smuggler
HOMEWORLD: Ando
SPECIES: Aqualish
HEIGHT: 1.7m (5ft 6in)
APPEARANCES: RO, IV
SEE ALSO: Doctor Evazan;
Obi-Wan Kenobi

Large eyes for
seeing underwater
on native planet

PONDA BABA is a thuggish
Aqualish who tries to pick a
fight with Luke Skywalker.
Luke enters a notorious Mos
Eisley cantina with Obi-Wan
Kenobi looking for a ride
off-planet. Ponda Baba's
big mistake is picking on
the companion of a Jedi.

Facial tusks
grow with age

PONDA BABA met
Dr. Evazan when he saved
the doctor's life. Together,
they shipped spice for
Jabba the Hutt. After the
fight in the cantina,
Evazan tries to use his
medical training to
reattach Ponda Baba's
arm but fails, nearly
killing the Aqualish in
the process.

Cantina Confrontation

Ponda Baba and his partner in crime,
Dr. Evazan, are caught unprepared for
an old man's ability with a lightsaber (an
almost forgotten relic of the glory days of
the Galactic Republic). But for Luke, too,
this first demonstration of Kenobi's abilities
with the weapon is a revelation, and
a hint of the possible return of the Jedi.

Teak Sidbam is a fellow
Aqualish who is sometimes
mistaken for Ponda Baba.

PRAETORIAN GUARD

SNOKE'S LAST LINE OF DEFENSE

DATA FILE

AFFILIATION: First Order
SPECIES: Human
STANDARD EQUIPMENT:
Bilari electro-chain whip;
electro-bisento; twin vibro-
arbir blades; vibro-voulge
APPEARANCES: VIII
SEE ALSO: Kylo Ren;
Supreme Leader Snoke

Twin vibro-arbir blades

Ever vigilant, the guards are
ready to leap into action
against Snoke's many enemies.

Segmented armor plates

THE RED clothing worn
by Praetorian Guards harks
back to the robes worn by
Emperor Palpatine's Royal
Guard. But these uniforms
have been upgraded to be
robust armor, able to deflect
even blaster fire.

THE PRAETORIAN GUARD
are eight sentries who
stand in Snoke's
throne room
aboard the
Supremacy.
They act as his
elite bodyguards.

Elegant Terror

These warriors battle in a unique martial-art
style with vibrating melee weapons that
bristle with electro-plasma energy. However,
they have never been truly tested against
those with formidable Force powers.

Armorweave robes

PRINCESS LEIA

GENERAL OF THE RESISTANCE

DATA FILE

AFFILIATION: Rebel Alliance/ Resistance
HOMEWORLD: Alderaan
SPECIES: Human
HEIGHT: 1.55m (5ft 1in)
APPEARANCES: III, RO, IV, V, VI, VII, VIII
SEE ALSO: Bail Organa; Han Solo; Luke Skywalker

AS SENATOR for Alderaan, Princess Leia Organa made diplomatic missions across the galaxy on her ship, the *Tantive IV*. Secretly, Leia worked for the Rebel Alliance, and she played a vital role in the defeat of the Empire.

Resistance uniform

RAISED ON Alderaan by
her adoptive father, Bail Organa, Leia was well prepared for her royal position, and used her high-placed connections wherever she could to aid the Alliance. During the decades of peace that follow the destruction of the Empire, Leia is able to concentrate on her new family, but as the galaxy once again undergoes turmoil, she returns to her role as a military commander.

Leia commands the Resistance from its base on D'Qar and then from her ship, the *Raddus*.

Decisive Leader

Leia was a key command figure in the Rebel Alliance, overseeing important missions and planning strategy, alongside General Rieekan and other Alliance leaders. In Echo Base on Hoth, Leia peered intently at the scanners, alert to any signs of Imperial detection.

Travel boots

PZ-4CO

COMMUNICATIONS DROID

DATA FILE

AFFILIATION: Resistance
TYPE: Communications droid
MANUFACTURER:
Serv-O-Droid
HEIGHT: 2.06m (6ft 8in)
APPEARANCES: VII, VIII
SEE ALSO: Admiral Statura;
C-3PO; Lieutenant Connix;
Princess Leia

Elongated neck

Data storage center

Intermotor actuating coupler

Fine manipulators

A CONSTANT FIXTURE in the Resistance base control rooms, PZ-4CO offers tactical data and communications support during important operations. She speaks in a pleasant, female voice.

THE PREVALENCE

of humanoid species in the galaxy has helped shape the forms of most protocol droids, as they are designed to mimic the life forms they interact with. PZ-4CO's anatomy is specifically modeled on the long-necked Tofallid species.

Intelligence Droids

PZ-4CO is one of many droids that form an invisible Resistance intelligence network. Droid agents scattered across the galaxy transmit reports back to Resistance headquarters, which PZ-4CO and C-3PO then assess in order to paint a real-time picture of First Order movements.

QI'RA

HAN SOLO'S FIRST LOVE

DATA FILE

AFFILIATION: Crimson Dawn
HOMEWORLD: Corellia
SPECIES: Human
HEIGHT: 1.58m (5ft 2in)
APPEARANCES: S
SEE ALSO: Dryden Vos;
Han Solo; Maul

QI'RA HAS COME a long way. Once a poor street urchin and scrumrat in the White Worms gang with Han Solo, she is now the right-hand lieutenant of the notorious crime boss Dryden Vos.

Moof-leather jacket with voorpak-fur lining

To get into the Kessel mines in a ploy to steal coaxium, Qi'ra pretends to be a slave trader.

QI'RA'S influential position with Dryden Vos serves her well, but working for Crimson Dawn is not a safe occupation. She navigates its dangerous waters with cunning and ruthlessness. To many, Qi'ra is just a pretty face, but her sparkling eyes are always on the prize. She patiently watches, listens, and waits.

Underestimated

Qi'ra kills Dryden Vos, and with him the shackles that tie her to Crimson Dawn. However, rather than making her escape, she reveals her true ambitions. She takes Vos' place in the organization with cool calculation, and reports directly to Maul.

QUEEN APAILANA

PADMÉ AMIDALA'S SUCCESSOR

Fan headdress worn in tribute to Padmé Amidala

THOUGH YOUNG, Queen Apailana has the qualities that the Naboo look for in their rulers: purity of heart and an absolute dedication to the peaceful values of the planet.

White makeup is ancient Naboo royal custom

Veda pearl suspensas

Cerlin capelet

QUEEN APAILANA is elected Queen of Naboo when she is just 12 years old. One of the youngest monarchs in the planet's history, she begins her reign toward the end of the Clone Wars.

Chersilk mourning robe

Thousands follow Padmé Amidala's funeral procession through Theed.

Standing strong

Queen Apailana is one of the chief mourners at Padmé Amidala's funeral on Naboo. Padmé had supported Apailana's bid for election. Although the official explanation for Padmé's death is that she died at the hands of renegade Jedi, Apailana privately believes otherwise.

QUI-GON JINN

JEDI WHO DISCOVERS "THE CHOSEN ONE"

DATA FILE

AFFILIATION: Jedi
HOMEWORLD: Coruscant
SPECIES: Human
HEIGHT: 1.93m (6ft 3in)
APPEARANCES: I
SEE ALSO: Anakin
Skywalker; Obi-Wan Kenobi

Qui-Gon Jinn is one of the
few Jedi to have battled
a Sith—Darth Maul.

Long hair worn back
to keep vision clear

QUI-GON JINN

is an experienced but
headstrong Jedi Master.
He was Padawan to Count
Dooku and teacher to
Obi-Wan Kenobi. Jinn has
sometimes clashed with
the Jedi High Council over
his favoring of risk and
action: as a result, he
has not been offered
a seat on the Council.

Jedi tunic

Jinn's dying wish is that
Obi-Wan trains Anakin.

The Chosen One

When Jinn encounters young Anakin
Skywalker, he believes he has discovered
the prophesized individual who will bring
balance to the Force. Jinn makes a bet
with slave owner Watto: if the boy wins
his podrace, then he also wins his freedom.
If he loses, Jinn loses his ship. The risk pays off,
and Jinn takes the boy to Coruscant to present
him to the Jedi High Council, with mixed results.

QUI-GON JINN

fights actively for the Galactic
Republic, but he is struck
down by the unruly dark
energies of Darth Maul. After
his death, Jinn becomes the
first Jedi to live on in the
Force, a gift he will pass on
to Obi-Wan Kenobi, Yoda,
and Anakin Skywalker.

Rugged travel boots

R2-D2

THE BRAVEST DROID IN THE GALAXY

DATA FILE

AFFILIATION: Republic/ Rebel Alliance/Resistance
TYPE: R-2 series astromech droid
MANUFACTURER: Industrial Automaton
HEIGHT: 1.09m (3ft 6in)
APPEARANCES: I, II, III, RO, IV, V, VI, VII, VIII
SEE ALSO: C-3PO; Luke Skywalker; Princess Leia

R2-D2 IS NO ORDINARY astromech droid. His long history of adventures has given him a distinct personality. He is stubborn and inventive, and is strongly motivated to succeed at any given task. Although R2-D2 speaks only in electronic beeps and whistles, he usually manages to make his point!

Holographic projector

R2-D2 has many hidden tricks, including extension arms and rocket boosters.

R2-D2

first distinguishes himself on board Queen Amidala's Royal Starship. He serves Anakin Skywalker during the Clone Wars and then Luke Skywalker during the Rebellion, flying in the droid socket of their starfighters.

Powerbus cables

Motorized, all-terrain treads

Risky Mission

At the end of the Clone Wars, R2-D2 is assigned to Bail Organa's diplomatic fleet. Princess Leia entrusts R2-D2 with the stolen Death Star plans and her urgent message to Obi-Wan Kenobi. He risks all kinds of damage to accomplish his mission.

R5-D4

ASTROMECH DROID SET TO DESTRUCT

R5-D4, ALSO KNOWN as "Red," is a white-and-red astromech droid that Jawas on Tatooine sell to Owen Lars. However, immediately after the sale, Red's motivator blows up, and Owen returns him to the Jawas. This gives C-3PO the opportunity he needs to recommend that Owen takes R2-D2 instead.

DATA FILE

AFFILIATION: None
TYPE: Astromech droid
MANUFACTURER: Industrial Automaton
HEIGHT: 97cm (3ft 2in)
APPEARANCES: II, IV
SEE ALSO: Jawa; Owen Lars; R2-D2

R5-D4 belongs to a series of droids that are cut-price versions of the superior R2 units. They are prone to defects and bad attitudes.

Photoreceptor

Panel conceals systems linkage and repair arms

Recharge coupling

Third tread for balance over uneven surfaces

Jawas hastily retrieve the inert R5-D4 from their disgusted customer.

Sabotage

What Owen and Luke do not know is that R2-D2 sabotaged R5-D4 when they were inside the Jawas' sandcrawler. Usually, droids' programming forbids them to mess with other droids, but Leia has instructed R2 to complete his mission at any cost.

FRONTIER STORMTROOPERS

DATA FILE

AFFILIATION: Empire
SPECIES: Human
STANDARD EQUIPMENT:
E-10R blaster rifles
APPEARANCES: S
SEE ALSO: Stormtroopers

IN AN EXPANDING Empire, new territories are hard to control. As soldiers push their way onto new planets, it is the job of range troopers to maintain rule on these distant, and often hostile, worlds.

Controls for integrated gription boots

Rugged E-10R blaster rifle

RANGE TROOPERS consider themselves the toughest of all the Imperial forces. These hardcore soldiers can withstand any environment. Their innate resilience is bolstered by extreme training, bespoke equipment, and ruthless determination to get the job done.

Kama lined with synth-fur

Security Duty

On Vandor, the Empire stores coaxium hyperspace fuel. Range troopers must ensure that the conveyex transports run to schedule—and arrive with their cargo still onboard.

Heavy-duty magnetomic gription boots can grip onto high-speed trains.

RAPPERTUNIE

MAX REBO BAND MEMBER

DATA FILE

AFFILIATION: Jabba's court
HOMEWORLD: Manpha
SPECIES: Shawda Ubb
HEIGHT: 30cm (12in)
APPEARANCES: VI
SEE ALSO: Max Rebo

RAPPERTUNIE plays a combination flute, or Growdi Harmonique, in Max Rebo's Band. Rappertunie has always had a thirst for travel and has used his musical talent to pay his way around the galaxy. Unfortunately, he ends up in a lifetime gig at Jabba's palace, where the hot, dry climate does not suit his moist skin at all.

Defense

At Jabba's palace, Rappertunie can spend whole days perched motionless on his Growdi seat, trying to keep his naturally moist skin cool. Being small in size makes Rappertunie feel quite vulnerable, but he can spit paralyzing poison at those who threaten him.

RAPPERTUNIE

is a Shawda Ubb—a small, amphibious species with long fingers. Rappertunie was born on the swampy, wet Outer Rim planet Manpha.

Naturally moist skin

Three fingers adapted for amphibious life on home planet

Growdi

Rappertunie plays away at the rear of the stage while secretly plotting his escape.

RAZOO QIN-FEE

KANJIKLUB GANGSTER

DATA FILE

AFFILIATION: Kanjiklub
HOMEWORLD: Nar Kanji
SPECIES: Human
HEIGHT: 1.65m (5ft 4in)
APPEARANCES: VII
SEE ALSO: Bala-Tik;
Chewbacca; Han Solo;
Kanjiklub gang; Tasu Leech

A LIEUTENANT in the cutthroat Kanjiklub gang, Razoo Qin-Fee specializes in weapons maintenance and modification. The bandits of Kanjiklub favor crude and deadly weaponry and explosives. Qin-Fee upgrades and modifies them to dangerous specifications.

Homemade explosive cylinders

Spare blaster gas ammunition cartridge

AUTHORITY IN

Kanjiklub is a violent affair—as is everything in this Outer Rim gang. Razoo Qin-Fee eyes the role of leader, currently held by Tasu Leech. However, he must make enough allies first, so that he is not instantly overthrown by others in the gang.

Razoo Qin-Fee accompanies Tasu Leech while boarding Han Solo's freighter, the *Eravana*, in an ill-fated attempt to collect money that Solo owes Kanjiklub.

Lethal Lieutenant

Razoo Qin-Fee earned a dangerous reputation in the underworld Zygerrian fighting circuit, where he was banned for exceptionally dirty tactics. Though he is a fierce, unarmed warrior, he is also a pyromaniac and tech expert. His extensively modified blaster rifle, which he has named the "Wasp," packs a powerful sting.

REBEL TROOPER

DATA FILE

AFFILIATION: Rebel Alliance
SPECIES: Human
STANDARD EQUIPMENT:
Blaster pistol
APPEARANCES: IV, V, VI, RO
SEE ALSO: General Madine

REBEL SOLDIERS are the main forces of the Alliance to Restore the Republic. These dedicated troops are organized into Sector Forces, each of which is responsible for resisting the might of the Empire in their home sectors across the galaxy.

A280-CFE
blaster rifle

Fleet troopers on the *Tantive IV* wear a uniform of blue shirts, black combat vests, and gray pants.

Cargo pants

REBEL TROOPS wear

standardized uniforms wherever the Alliance's meager resources allow. SpecForce wilderness fighters— soldiers trained for specialized roles in Alliance Special Forces— wear full forest-camouflaged fatigues during the Battle of Endor.

Commandos

Alliance SpecForce wilderness fighters infiltrate an Imperial base on Endor's forest moon. Under the command of General Solo, they manage to trick the squadrons of Imperial troops inside the base to come out, where they are outnumbered and forced to surrender.

Heavy-
duty boots

REY

DATA FILE

AFFILIATION: Resistance
HOMEWORLD: Jakku
SPECIES: Human
HEIGHT: 1.7m (5ft 6in)
APPEARANCES: VII, VIII
SEE ALSO: BB-8; Finn;
Kylo Ren; Luke
Skywalker

Lightsaber
was Luke's
and, before
that, Anakin's

A 19-YEAR-OLD scavenger who lives in the inhospitable deserts of Jakku, Rey never intends to leave the desolate planet. Then a chance encounter catapults her into galactic adventures.

REY IS SURPRISED to learn that she has a vital role to play in the fate of the galaxy. She struggles to find her place in it all and is torn between the light and dark sides of the Force —and between Luke Skywalker and Kylo Ren.

Rey is the first person in many years to see Luke Skywalker when she tracks him down on the remote planet of Ahch-To.

First Order Refuser

Despite a hard life that should have left Rey free of sympathy and compassion, she looks for the best in people. She believes there is good in Kylo Ren and tries to reason with him. Together, they survive an encounter with Snoke and his Praetorian Guard, but Rey then refuses to join Ren when it becomes clear he is intent on a darker path than she is willing to follow.

**Jakku gauze wraps
combined with
Jedi-style tunic**

RIO DURANT

DATA FILE

AFFILIATION: Tobias Beckett's crew, Crimson Dawn
HOMEWORLD: Ardennia
SPECIES: Ardennian
HEIGHT: 1.49m (4ft 9in)
APPEARANCES: S
SEE ALSO: Han Solo; Tobias Beckett; Val

Red-tinted flying goggles

Torplex LVD-41 pilot life-support kit

Toes can grasp tools and controls

Rio tells a great story round the campfire, reliving crazy capers with all four of his arms.

A FOUR-ARMED Ardennian pilot, Rio earned his wings with the Freedom Sons, fighting alongside the Republic in the Clone Wars. Now he uses his military skills in Tobias Beckett's criminal crew.

GENIAL RIO is good to have around in tense or dangerous situations. He lifts morale with jokes and stories. He is up for any scam, such as pretending to be choked by Beckett to clear a gaming table. He also loves to cook, which goes down well with teammates at the end of a long day.

Rio and Han

Rio is not sure about Han Solo joining the team at first, but he is won over in the end. He is glad to have Han with him when he is shot by a Cloud-Rider during the coaxium heist on Vandor. Rio's death makes a deep impression on Han and strengthens his resolve to find his long-lost love, Qi'ra.

ROSE TICO

HEROIC MECHANIC

DATA FILE

AFFILIATION: Resistance
HOMEWORLD: Hays Minor
SPECIES: Human
HEIGHT: Unknown
APPEARANCES: VIII
SEE ALSO: DJ; Finn; Paige Tico

ROSE TICO spends her days below decks as a maintenance worker aboard the *Raddus*. She never imagined she would meet a hero of the Resistance like Finn, yet alone join him on a daring mission across the galaxy.

AFTER experiencing the brutality of the First Order on their home planet, Rose and her sister, Paige, joined the Resistance. It was Paige who gave Rose her sense of right and wrong and taught her to never give up. Rose's technical skills and logical mind prove very valuable to the Resistance.

Identification plaque

Mechanic's overalls

Coded override data spikes

Rose is starstruck to meet Finn, but she is equally capable when they go on a mission.

Fathier Freer

A harsh life has not hardened Rose to others' suffering. When she sees the cruel captivity of the fathiers in Canto Bight, she frees them. This kindness is repaid by one of the majestic beasts, who helps her and Finn get away.

Electro-shock prod for stopping deserters

RYSTÁLL

PERFORMER IN THE MAX REBO BAND

DATA FILE

AFFILIATION: Jabba's court
HOMEWORLD: Coruscant
SPECIES: Half Theelin/
half human
HEIGHT: 1.7m (5ft 6in)
APPEARANCES: III, VI
SEE ALSO: Greeata; Lyn Me

RYSTÁLL SANT'S adoptive parents are Ortolan musicians from Coruscant. They arrange for their dazzling daughter to perform as a singer and dancer with Max Rebo's band, where she will turn heads.

Natural markings highlighted with stage makeup

Rystáll and fellow singer Greeata are shocked by the depravities they witness at Jabba's palace.

RYSTÁLL IS part-human and part-Theelin. The Theelin are a rare species with head horns, brightly colored hair, and mottled skin. Rystáll also has hooved feet. Many Theelin have artistic personalities and choose to become artists or performers.

Cape is a gift from a passing admirer, Syrh Rhoams

Dancer's graceful body

Hooves

Star Attraction

The colorful Rystáll Sant has always attracted the attention of a variety of characters, including the high-placed lieutenant in the criminal Black Sun organization, who tricked her into slavery. Lando Calrissian later freed her. At Jabba's palace she attracts the attention of bounty hunter Boba Fett.

SABÉ

ROYAL NABOO HANDMAIDEN

DATA FILE

AFFILIATION: Royal House of Naboo
HOMEWORLD: Naboo
SPECIES: Human
HEIGHT: 1.65m (5ft 4in)
APPEARANCES: I
SEE ALSO: Padmé Amidala

Royal headdress

Scar of remembrance

SABÉ IS THE MOST important handmaiden in Queen Amidala's entourage. She is first in line to become the royal decoy in times of danger. Sabé dresses as the queen and disguises her features with white makeup.

Broad waistband

Surcoat

QUEEN AMIDALA'S
handmaidens assist with many tasks necessary to maintain the monarch's regal image. These capable individuals are also trained in bodyguard skills and are equipped with blaster pistols to defend their monarch in the event of a disturbance or emergency.

Long battle-dress made of blast-damping fabric

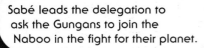

Sabé leads the delegation to ask the Gungans to join the Naboo in the fight for their planet.

Royal Service
While Sabé is disguised as the queen, Padmé Amidala dresses in the simple gown of a handmaiden. They use silent gestures and expressions to communicate secretly with each other. Sabé is trained to imitate the queen in every way, but the task is a risky one.

SAESEE TIIN

IKTOTCHI JEDI MASTER

DATA FILE

AFFILIATION: Jedi
HOMEWORLD: Iktotch
SPECIES: Iktotchi
HEIGHT: 1.88m (6ft 2in)
APPEARANCES: I, II, III
SEE ALSO: Mace Windu

JEDI MASTER SAESEE TIIN sits on the High Council in the Jedi Temple on Coruscant. He is particularly skilled in piloting the finest spacecraft at high speeds, which is also when his telepathic mind does its most focused thinking.

Well-developed horns

Lightsaber

Tough skin protects against high winds of Iktotchon

Customary humanoid Jedi robes

SAESEE TIIN was born on Iktotch, the moon of Iktotchon. He is a natural pilot, exhibiting an instinctive sense of direction and a fine control of ships of many different sizes. During an important Clone Wars mission to Lola Sayu, the site of the Separatist Citadel installation, Tiin pilots his well-maintained starfighter into battle.

Jedi Fighter

Saesee Tiin fights at the Battle of Geonosis, riding on a Republic gunship to attack the droids on the plains. Later in the battle, Tiin takes to the skies to aid Jedi Master Adi Gallia in the battle above Geonosis. Tiin becomes a general in the Clone Wars, leading starfighter squadrons.

Tiin is one of the Jedi who confront Palpatine, now revealed to be Sidious.

SALACIOUS CRUMB

KOWAKIAN MONKEY-LIZARD

DATA FILE

AFFILIATION: Jabba's court
HOMEWORLD: Kowak
SPECIES: Kowakian monkey-lizard
HEIGHT: 70cm (2ft 3in)
APPEARANCES: VI
SEE ALSO: Jabba the Hutt

SALACIOUS CRUMB is Jabba the Hutt's court jester. When Jabba first found this Kowakian monkey-lizard stealing his food, the Hutt tried to eat him. Crumb escaped but Bib Fortuna captured him.

Highly sensitive ears

Hooked reptilian beak

Collar of scruffy fur

Spindly arm

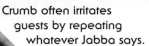

Crumb often irritates guests by repeating whatever Jabba says.

In Jest

Salacious Crumb knows that he must make Jabba laugh at least once a day, otherwise he will be killed. Crumb picks on everyone around him to entertain his boss, especially Jabba's new translator droid, C-3PO, who loses an eye to the hateful little creature.

SALACIOUS CRUMB

was just one of the many vermin on a space station, until he managed to stow away on board one of Jabba's spaceships, ending up on Tatooine. Now Crumb sits beside Jabba the Hutt, teasing all the inhabitants of the palace.

Sharp talons

SANDTROOPER

DESERT-READY STORMTROOPERS

DATA FILE

AFFILIATION: Empire
SPECIES: Human
HEIGHT: 1.83m (6ft)
STANDARD EQUIPMENT:
Blaster pistol; blaster rifle;
repeating blaster
APPEARANCES: IV, RO
SEE ALSO: Stormtrooper

SANDTROOPERS are specialized Imperial stormtroopers, trained to adapt to desert environments. They are equipped with armor and weapons for use in hot, dry climates. Their armor uses advanced cooling systems and their helmets have built-in polarized lenses to reduce sun glare.

Pauldron indicates rank

SD-48 survival backpack

Utility belt

Ranks

Sandtroopers wear shoulder pauldrons, which indicate rank. Regular sandtroopers' pauldrons are black, while sergeants wear white pauldrons. Squad leaders, who lead units of seven troopers, wear orange pauldrons.

SANDTROOPERS

are human recruits who remain anonymous behind their white armor. They carry food and water supplies, blaster rifles, and long-range comlinks. Sandtroopers' training enables them to adapt to local customs, like riding native dewback lizards on Tatooine.

177

SARCO PLANK

DATA FILE

AFFILIATION: None
HOMEWORLD: Unknown
SPECIES: Melitto
HEIGHT: 1.82m (6ft)
APPEARANCES: VII
SEE ALSO: Luke Skywalker;
C-3PO; Unkar Plutt; Rey

Vocoder helmet

Nutrient and
fluid dispenser

A SCAVENGER and bounty hunter, the sinister Sarco Plank works as an arms trader at Niima Outpost on Jakku, where he sells weapons to explorers willing to brave the desert wastes in search of valuable salvage.

DURING the Galactic Civil War, Sarco worked as a tomb raider, robbing ancient sites such as the Temple of Eedit, a Jedi outpost on Devaron. In that expedition, Sarco lured a young Luke Skywalker to the temple, hoping the youth could unlock the site's secrets. Sarco fought Luke, wielding an electrostaff against Skywalker's lightsaber, but failed to defeat the rebel pilot.

Eyeless Alien

Sarco Plank lacks eyes—his face is a featureless wall of insectoid plates. He senses his surroundings based on vibrations transmitted by ultra-sensitive hairs known as cilia, which line his body. A vocoder built into his feeding mask translates the humming of his face plates into an understandable voice.

SAW GERRERA

BATTLE-DAMAGED WARRIOR

DATA FILE

AFFILIATION: His own splinter group
HOMEWORLD: Onderon
SPECIES: Human
HEIGHT: 1.8m (5ft 9in)
APPEARANCES: RO
SEE ALSO: Bodhi Rook; Jyn Erso

CONSIDERED TOO extreme even for the Rebel Alliance, Saw Gerrera sets up his own ragtag militia. His obsession to stop the Empire comes at any cost, often even endangering civilians.

GERRERA'S will to fight is strong, but his body is weak. He wears a pressurized suit to help him breathe. What is left of his warrior's body is flooded with dangerous levels of medicine. It is dispensed to him by G2-1B7, a medical droid that he has reprogrammed to bypass safety levels.

Breathing tube

Dxunwood walking stick

Old Onderonian banner worn as a cape

Gerrera raised Jyn from the age of eight, as part of his criminal cell.

Cybernetic foot plate

Suspicious Gerrera

Gerrera's distrust has developed into paranoia in his old age. When an Imperial pilot defects to him, he cannot trust his motives. After using the tentacled Bor Gullet to read the pilot's mind—even at the possible cost of his sanity—Gerrera is still convinced that the pilot is a trap.

SCOUT TROOPER

SPECIALIZED STORMTROOPERS

DATA FILE

AFFILIATION: Empire
SPECIES: Human
STANDARD EQUIPMENT:
Blaster pistol; grenades;
survival rations and gear
APPEARANCES: VI
SEE ALSO: Sandtrooper;
stormtrooper

IMPERIAL SCOUT TROOPERS

are trained for long-term missions.
They wear armor on their head
and upper body only, to allow
maximum maneuverability.
Their helmets have enhanced
macrobinocular viewplates,
for precision target
identification.

Survival rations

SCOUT TROOPERS

are sent to survey areas and
locate enemy positions, infiltrate
enemy territory, and undertake
sabotage missions. They rarely
engage in combat, and are
instructed to call in stormtroopers
at any signs of trouble.

Body glove

The Republic first deployed
clone scout troopers during
the Clone Wars, including
at the Battle of Kachirho
on Kashyyyk.

Pistol holder

On Patrol

Scout troopers on speeder bikes
patrol the dense forests of Endor,
where the Empire maintains a
strategic shield generator. Working
in units of two or four, they watch
for any signs of troublesome forest
creatures or terrorist infiltrators.

SEBULBA

SEBULBA IS ONE of the top podracers in the Outer Rim circuits. He is skilled at piloting his vehicle, but also willing to use dirty tricks to give him the winning edge. When Anakin Skywalker joins a race, Sebulba decides the young human must not win.

DATA FILE

AFFILIATION: None
HOMEWORLD: Malastare
SPECIES: Dug
HEIGHT: 1.12m (3ft 7in)
APPEARANCES: I
SEE ALSO: Anakin Skywalker

Grasping hands

Race goggles

Beaded danglers

Sebulba pilots a giant orange podracer with many secret weapons concealed in it.

SEBULBA

is a Dug from Malastare, a species notorious for being bullies. Playing up to his tough, violent image for the crowds, Sebulba wears a flashy, custom-designed leather racing suit.

Leather wrist guard

Trophy coins

Although Sebulba crashes during the Boonta Eve Classic, he survives to race in other competitions.

Dangerous Driver

The dastardly Dug gives himself the winning edge in races by sabotaging other racers. Sebulba can pull up alongside another podracer and blast it with his hidden flame thrower, or throw concussion weapons into another pilot's cockpit.

Tight leather leg-straps

SHAAK TI

TOGRUTA JEDI MASTER

Characteristic pigmentation of the Togruta species

JEDI MASTER SHAAK TI joined the Jedi High Council before the arena battle on Geonosis. During the Clone Wars, she often represents the Jedi Order on Kamino. Her compassion for the clone troopers as individuals clashes with the Kaminoan scientists' cold view that they are products.

Hollow montrals sense space

Two-handed grip for control

Jedi robe

Shaak Ti is the same species as Anakin Skywalker's apprentice, Ahsoka Tano.

Master Jedi

Shaak Ti fights alongside the other 200 Jedi Knights that come to the aid of Anakin Skywalker, Obi-Wan Kenobi, and Padmé Amidala on Geonosis. After the conflict in the arena, she boards a Republic gunship for the front lines of the battle against the massed droid army.

TOGRUTA Shaak Ti is one of the best Jedi fighters in group combat. Her hollow head montrals sense space ultrasonically, sharpening her spatial awareness. Where others struggle with the complexity of movements, Shaak Ti darts with ease.

SHMI SKYWALKER

ANAKIN SKYWALKER'S MOTHER

Simple hairstyle typical of servants

SHMI SKYWALKER HAS lived a hard life as a slave since pirates captured her parents when she was a girl. Owned by junk dealer Watto on Tatooine, Shmi gives birth to a child named Anakin, who also works as a slave.

Decorative belt

IN SPITE OF her poverty, Shmi tries to give Anakin a good home in the slave quarter of Mos Espa. Anakin's departure is hard for Shmi to bear, but she comes to live a happier life when a settler farmer, Cliegg Lars, frees her in order to marry her.

Rough-spun tunic withstands harsh Tatooine weather

Shmi refuses to let her love for Anakin keep him from what she feels is his destiny—to be a Jedi.

Tragic Loss

When Anakin Skywalker senses that his mother is in terrible pain, he travels to Tatooine to help her. However, he cannot prevent her death at the hands of the Sand People. Experiencing great anger and pain, Anakin vows to build his power until nothing can withstand it.

Simple skirt

SHOCK TROOPER

MEMBERS OF THE CORUSCANT GUARD

DATA FILE

AFFILIATION:
Republic/Empire
HOMEWORLD: Kamino
SPECIES: Human clone
HEIGHT: 1.83m (6ft)
APPEARANCES: II, III
SEE ALSO: Stormtrooper

AS THE REPUBLIC PREPARES for war, red-emblazoned shock troopers begin to patrol public spaces on Coruscant, to ensure public order and security. They also serve as bodyguards for politicians, including Supreme Chancellor Palpatine.

Upgraded breath filter and annunciator

Coruscant designation

Shock-absorbing plastoid armor

D15 rifle

In the last days of the Republic, people begin to refer to shock troopers as stormtroopers.

SHOCK TROOPERS

are members of the Coruscant Guard. Palpatine set up the unit to strengthen the Coruscant Security Force and the Senate Guard. Shock troopers keep watch on government buildings and landing platforms.

Palpatine's Guard

Shock troopers go with Palpatine to the Senate after the Jedi's failed attempt to arrest him. After Yoda's battle with Palpatine, they unsuccessfully search for the Jedi Master's body. Shock troopers also accompany Palpatine to Mustafar, where they find Darth Vader's burned body.

SHORETROOPER

BEACH STORMTROOPERS

DATA FILE

AFFILIATION: Empire
SPECIES: Human
HEIGHT: 1.83m (6ft)
STANDARD EQUIPMENT:
E-22 blaster rifle
APPEARANCES: RO
SEE ALSO: Stormtrooper

Air filter

SHORETROOPERS stand out against the plain-white armor of regular stormtroopers, and blend in with sand and palm tree trunks. They are specially trained and equipped for tropical planets like Scarif, which houses the high-security Citadel complex.

Blue chest markings show rank of captain

Belt contains ammunition for blaster weapons

MOST shoretroopers are sergeants, so would have operational command over regular stormtroopers. However, Scarif is such a fortified planet that few people expect an attack to ever come close to the Citadel.

Shoretroopers are ready to face the unexpected, such as rebels inside the perimeter.

Beach Ready

Shoretroopers are equipped for their environment. Fans in their helmets keep them cool and air filters reduce sand inhalation. Temperature-controlled bodysuits are sealed under lightweight armor, which has a special coating to prevent salt damage from the sea air.

Leg armor expands

SHU MAI

PRESIDENT OF THE COMMERCE GUILD

DATA FILE

AFFILIATION: Commerce Guild, Separatists
HOMEWORLD: Castell
SPECIES: Gossam
HEIGHT: 1.65m (5ft 4in)
APPEARANCES: II, III
SEE ALSO: Count Dooku; Nute Gunray; Wat Tambor

Shu Mai awaits her fate on volcanic Mustafar with the rest of the Separatist leaders.

Neck rings

Emblazoned jewel crest

SHU MAI IS PRESIDENT of the powerful Commerce Guild, whose forces fight the Republic during the Clone Wars. Mai is a member of the Separatist Council alongside Nute Gunray, Wat Tambor, and others. She is obsessed with status and power.

Rich skirt made of rare uris silk

SHU MAI is a Gossam from the planet Castell. She is only concerned with status, power, and wealth. Mai worked her way up the Commerce Guild using aggressive and unscrupulous tactics, until no rivals stood in her way to becoming president.

Gossams have three-toed feet

Sneaky Practices

Shu Mai is not the only Separatist leader to pledge her support to Dooku in secret, knowing that it amounts to treason. Though the Commerce Guild does not openly back the Separatists, Shu Mai's homing spider droids begin to fight on the battlefields of the Clone Wars.

SIO BIBBLE

GOVERNOR OF NABOO

SIO BIBBLE is Governor of Naboo during the Trade Federation invasion. He oversees all matters brought to Queen Amidala's attention. He also chairs the Advisory Council, the governing body of Naboo. Sio is completely opposed to violence.

Formal collar

Fashionable Naboo sleeves and cuffs

Philosopher's tunic

DATA FILE

AFFILIATION: Royal House of Naboo
HOMEWORLD: Naboo
SPECIES: Human
HEIGHT: 1.7m (5ft 6in)
APPEARANCES: I, II, III
SEE ALSO: Captain Panaka; Nute Gunray; Padmé Amidala

BIBBLE IS A

philosopher who was elected governor under Amidala's predecessor, King Veruna. Sio is initially critical of Amidala, but comes to respect her. He later serves under Amidala's successors, Queens Jamillia, Neeyutnee, and Apailana.

Bibble refuses to accept Captain Panaka's warnings of greater need for armament.

Under Arrest

During the invasion of Naboo, battle droids arrest Sio Bibble and Queen Amidala. When two Jedi Knights rescue Amidala, the governor chooses to stay with his people. Bibble leads them in a hunger strike, and earns the ire of the Trade Federation Viceroy, Nute Gunray.

Governor's boots

SLY MOORE

PALPATINE'S STAFF AIDE

Eyes see only in ultraviolet light

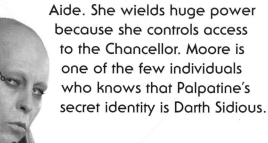

SLY MOORE is Palpatine's Staff Aide. She wields huge power because she controls access to the Chancellor. Moore is one of the few individuals who knows that Palpatine's secret identity is Darth Sidious.

Umbarans conceal their emotions

DATA FILE

AFFILIATION: Republic
HOMEWORLD: Umbara
SPECIES: Umbaran
HEIGHT: 1.78m (5ft 8in)
APPEARANCES: II, III
SEE ALSO: Chancellor Valorum; Palpatine

Sly Moore often attends Palpatine's meetings, silently shadowing the Supreme Chancellor.

SLY MOORE is an Umbaran—a technologically advanced species from Umbara. This planet is known as "the Shadow World" because so little natural light reaches its surface. Umbarans are known for their ability to use their minds to subtly influence, and control, others.

Power Play

In Palpatine's administration, Sly Moore holds the post that Sei Taria had in Chancellor Valorum's time. Some whisper that Moore must have threatened the committed and dedicated Sei Taria with blackmail to persuade her to stand down.

Umbaran shadow cloak is patterned in ultraviolet colors

SNAP WEXLEY

RESISTANCE RECON PILOT

DATA FILE

AFFILIATION: Resistance
HOMEWORLD: Akiva
SPECIES: Human
HEIGHT: 1.88m (6ft 2in)
APPEARANCES: VII
SEE ALSO: Jess Pava; Poe Dameron; Princess Leia

A SKILLED X-wing pilot serving in Blue Squadron, Temmin "Snap" Wexley is a captain in the Resistance, and recognized by Poe Dameron as the best recon flier in the force.

FrieTek life-support unit

Inflatable life vest

Flight helmet

Snap is said to have a keen eye for trouble and the piloting skills to evade it.

AFTER THE STARKILLER

weapon destroys the New Republic's capital world, Resistance controllers are able to triangulate its location. Snap Wexley flies a daring recon mission into the Unknown Regions, and records vital information about the secret base that allows the Resistance to formulate an attack strategy.

Rebel Roots

The son of Norra Wexley, a veteran Y-wing pilot who flew at the Battle of Endor, Snap hails from Akiva, an Outer Rim world that was an Imperial base prior to its liberation by the New Republic. At that time, young Wexley learned street-smarts and survived with the help of his protector, a modified battle droid named Mister Bones.

SNOWTROOPER

EXTREME-CLIMATE STORMTROOPERS

DATA FILE

AFFILIATION: Empire
SPECIES: Human
HEIGHT: 1.83m (6ft)
STANDARD EQUIPMENT: E-11 blaster rifle; light repeating blasters; grenades
APPEARANCES: V
SEE ALSO: Shock trooper

Polarized snow goggles

IMPERIAL SNOWTROOPERS

are specialized stormtroopers that form self-sufficient mobile combat units in environments of snow and ice. Their backpacks and suit systems keep their bodies warm, while their face masks are equipped with breath heaters.

E-11 blaster rifle

THE EMPIRE modeled its snowtroopers on the Galactic Republic's specialized clone cold assault troopers, who fought in the Clone Wars on frozen worlds such as Orto Plutonia.

Storage pouch

Insulated belt cape

Snowtroopers carry and set up deadly E-web heavy repeating blasters in snowy terrain.

Rugged ice boots

Assault on Hoth

Snowtroopers are deployed as part of General Veers's Blizzard Force at the Battle of Hoth. Snowtroopers work in tandem with AT-AT walkers to effect a massive strike. They defeat the forces of the Rebel Alliance and break into Echo Base. These specialized soldiers can survive for two weeks in extreme cold terrain on suit battery power alone.

STASS ALLIE

THOLOTHIAN JEDI MASTER

Tholoth headdress

Common lightsaber design

THOLOTHIAN Jedi Master Stass Allie serves the Republic during the Clone Wars. As the cousin of a highly distinguished Jedi, Adi Gallia, Allie is keen to demonstrate her own abilities. After Gallia's death in the Clone Wars, Allie takes her place on the Jedi Council.

Utility belt

Stass Allie patrols Saleucami on a speeder bike, where she will lose her life to Order 66.

STASS ALLIE is a formidable warrior, but her talent for healing is even more impressive. Allie passes on her healing expertise to others among the Jedi Order—including Barriss Offee.

Tall travel boots

Brave Fighter

Joining Mace Windu's Jedi task force to Geonosis, Stass Allie participates in the arena battle. She is one of the few survivors, continuing to fight as the battle escalates outside the arena.

STORMTROOPER

THE EMPIRE'S ELITE SOLDIERS

DATA FILE

AFFILIATION: Empire
SPECIES: Human
HEIGHT: 1.83m (6ft)
STANDARD EQUIPMENT:
E-11 blaster rifle; thermal detonator
APPEARANCES: S, RO, IV, V, VI
SEE ALSO: Snowtrooper

STORMTROOPERS ARE THE most effective troops in the Imperial military and the most feared opponents of the Rebel Alliance. They are highly disciplined and completely loyal to the Emperor, carrying out commands without hesitation.

Blaster power cell container

STORMTROOPERS

are human recruits who remain anonymous behind their white armor. This armor protects them from harsh environments and glancing shots from blaster bolts.

Reinforced alloy plate ridge

Sniper position knee protector plate

The massed ranks of disciplined stormtroopers obey their orders unquestioningly.

Fight to Win

In battle, stormtroopers are disciplined to ignore casualties within their own ranks. Notice is only taken from a tactical standpoint. Stormtroopers are never distracted by emotional responses.

Positive-grip boots

SUPER BATTLE DROID

UPGRADED BATTLE DROID

DATA FILE

AFFILIATION: Separatists
TYPE: B2 super battle droid
MANUFACTURER: Baktoid
Combat Automata
HEIGHT: 1.93m (6ft 3in)
APPEARANCES: II, III
SEE ALSO: Battle droid

Arms stronger
than battle
droid limbs

Monogrip
hands are hard
to damage

AFTER THE TRADE FEDERATION'S
defeat in the Battle of Naboo, its leaders
commissioned an improved battle droid.
Tough and heavily armed, super
battle droids break Republic
regulations on private security
forces. However, the Neimoidians
have too much influence to care.

THE DROID
foundries of Geonosis
secretly manufacture
super battle droids.
The droids have
standard battle droid
internal components
for economy, but
they utilize a much
stronger shell.

Flexible
armored
midsection

Excess
heat radiated
through calf vanes

Fearless Droids
Super battle droids can be poor at
formulating attack plans. However,
they make up for this lack by their
fearlessness in battle, reducing
their targets to ruins.

Strap-on foot tips
can be replaced
with claws or pads

R2-D2 has his own way of fighting
super battle droids: he shoots oil
at them, before setting them on fire.

ARCHITECT OF THE FIRST ORDER

DATA FILE

AFFILIATION: First Order
HOMEWORLD: Unknown
SPECIES: Unknown
HEIGHT: More than 2.1m
(6ft 3in)
APPEARANCES: VII, VIII
SEE ALSO: General Hux;
Kylo Ren; Praetorian Guard

Scar channel

Sunken face caused
by malformed bone

LIFE UNDER Supreme Leader Snoke's First Order is cruel and terrifying. The dictator's every whim is enforced without question by a high-tech, well-trained army of stormtroopers.

Snoke believes that Kylo Ren's Skywalker ancestry makes him the key to wiping out the Jedi.

Master of Manipulation

Snoke understands the power of fear and reputation, so he is rarely seen in person. Instead, he gives orders via hologram. His enlarged, grotesque image comes across as even more monstrous than he is in the flesh.

ALTHOUGH he is not a Sith, Snoke has many Force abilities. He has mastered telepathy, mind probing, telekinesis, Force-choke, and Force lightning. Following ancient Sith traditions, he also takes an apprentice, Kylo Ren. Snoke exploits Ren's weaknesses so that he will do Snoke's bidding for him.

Extravagant
gold-flecked robes

SY SNOOTLES

LEAD VOCALIST FOR THE MAX REBO BAND

DATA FILE

AFFILIATION: Jabba's court
HOMEWORLD: Lowick
SPECIES: Pa'lowick
HEIGHT: 1.6m (5ft 3in)
APPEARANCES: VI
SEE ALSO: Max Rebo; Greeata

Expressive mouth

Retractable tusks protrude from second mouth

Powerful chest for swimming— and singing!

Pa'lowicks have lean limbs, round bodies, eye-stalks, and long lip-stalks.

Skin coloration provides camouflage in swamps of homeworld

SY SNOOTLES IS A

Pa'lowick singer and lead vocalist for the Max Rebo Band when they played at Jabba's palace. Snootles only agrees to join the band on the strict condition that Rebo also hires her good friend, Greeata Jendowanian, as a dancer and singer.

SNOOTLES has had an adventurous life. She used to be Ziro the Hutt's lover but then, on discovering the true extent of his cruelty, became his assassin. In Jabba's palace, Snootles works as a double-agent, feeding Bib Fortuna's lies to Jabba's enemies.

Microphone stand

Forward and backward-facing toes for walking on shallow lakes

Strange Singing

Jabba's appreciation of Sy Snootles's singing has given her a vastly inflated idea of her own talent. When the band splits up after Jabba's death, Snootles finds it hard to make it anywhere mainstream—the chief reason being her vocals are just too weird.

TALLISSAN "TALLIE" LINTRA

BLUE LEADER AT D'QAR

DATA FILE

AFFILIATION: Resistance, Blue Squadron
HOMEWORLD: Pippip 3
SPECIES: Human
HEIGHT: 1.73m (5ft 8in)
APPEARANCES: VIII
SEE ALSO: Paige Tico; Poe Dameron

TALLIE LINTRA'S flying career began with spraying crops on her parents' farm in a RZ-1 A-wing adapted into a cropduster. Now she flies a RZ-2 A-wing for the Resistance and is one of their finest pilots.

Synthsilk scarf was a gift from her father

Standard-issue green flight suit

TALLIE proves herself to be a highly capable pilot, impressing even Poe Dameron with her skills. Her role in the Resistance is varied. She flies relief missions, defends larger craft, attacks targets, and engages in dogfights with First Order TIE fighters.

Blue One

During the Evacuation of D'Qar, Squadron Leader Lintra flies as Blue One, leading Blue Squadron. The starfighters escort and cover the MG-100 StarFortress bombers that contain enough firepower to bring down the *Fulminatrix*—the entire First Order Dreadnought.

Tallie is revved up, about to take off from the *Raddus* hangar when it is hit by shots from Kylo Ren's TIE silencer.

Guidenhauser ejection harness

TANK TROOPER

DATA FILE

AFFILIATION: Empire
SPECIES: Human
HEIGHT: 1.83m (6ft)
STANDARD VEHICLE:
TX-225 "Occupier" combat
assault tank
APPEARANCES: RO
SEE ALSO: Stormtrooper

TANK TROOPERS are stormtroopers trained for Imperial ground assault vehicles. One assignment could be ferrying troops in huge transports. The next could be leading an assault in a heavily armed tank.

Air filter

Lightweight armor for squeezing in a tank

Tanks carry looted kyber crystals out of Jedha City so they can be sent offworld.

A TRIO of terror, tank troopers work in teams of three: a driver, a gunner, and a tank commander on top. The driver is also responsible for the tank's maintenance.

Sitting Ducks

Bulky TX-225 tanks are a strong statement of power, but they also make troopers an easy target for rebellious locals. And there is no quick way out of Jedha's winding streets.

TARFFUL

WOOKIEE CHIEFTAIN

Teeth bared for war cry

DATA FILE

AFFILIATION: Republic
HOMEWORLD: Kashyyyk
SPECIES: Wookiee
HEIGHT: 2.34m (7ft 7in)
APPEARANCES: III
SEE ALSO: Chewbacca

TARFFUL IS LEADER of the Wookiee city of Kachirho. When the Separatist forces invade his planet, Kashyyyk, Tarfful works with Chewbacca and Jedi Yoda, Luminara Unduli, and Quinlan Vos to plan the Wookiees' strategy for repelling the invaders.

Decorative pauldron

Orb-igniter

Tarfful and Chewbacca help Yoda flee in a hidden escape pod after Order 66.

TARFFUL WAS

once enslaved by the Trandoshan slavers, who have long been the enemies of the Wookiees. When clone troops rescued him, Tarfful pledged to fight anyone who tried to enslave his people or capture his planet.

Thick calf muscles from climbing trees

Fur protects upper foot

Wookiee Attack

Tarfful is a calm, considerate Wookiee who can be a mighty warrior when necessary. He leads his fellow Wookiees in daring raids on amphibious Separatist tank droids.

TASU LEECH

KANJIKLUB LEADER

DATA FILE

AFFILIATION: Kanjiklub
HOMEWORLD: Nar Kanji
SPECIES: Human
HEIGHT: 1.57m (5ft 2in)
APPEARANCES: VII
SEE ALSO: Chewbacca;
Han Solo; Kanjiklub gang;
Razoo Qin-Fee

TASU LEECH IS the current leader of the notorious Kanjiklub gang. He is an unruly street fighter who firmly holds on to his position by showing no signs of weakness.

Plastoid blast jerkin

Spare ammunition

TASU LEECH

grew up on Nar Kanji, on the frontiers of the galaxy, and clawed his way to the top of the Kanjiklub. He refuses to speak Basic, considering it a weak language of cowardly people.

"Huttsplitter" blaster rifle

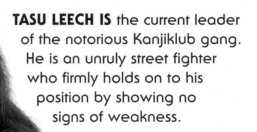

Deal Gone Bad

Solo has twice before failed to deliver cargo to Kanjiklub, shortening Tasu's already violent temper. Boarding Solo's freighter in search of compensation, Tasu's standoff with Solo turns deadly when a shipment of rathtars escape, sending Kanjiklubbers scurrying for their lives.

TEEBO

EWOK MYSTIC

DATA FILE

AFFILIATION: Bright Tree Village
HOMEWORLD: Forest moon of Endor
SPECIES: Ewok
HEIGHT: 1.24m (4ft 1in)
APPEARANCES: VI
SEE ALSO: Chief Chirpa; Logray

Churi feathers

Gurreck skull headdress

Teebo joins the Rebel Alliance with his fellow Ewoks to defeat the Imperial army on Endor.

Authority stick

Striped pelt

THE EWOK NAMED

Teebo is a watcher of the stars and a poet. Teebo has a mystical connection to the forces of nature. His keen perceptive abilities and practical thinking have made Teebo a leading figure within his tribe.

TEEBO had many adventures growing up in his tribe before becoming an apprentice of the tribal shaman, Logray. He is learning the ways of Ewok magic and hopes to become the Ewok shaman someday.

Aggressive Beginnings

When Teebo first sees Han Solo and his team, he distrusts them. After being freed from his bonds, R2-D2 promptly zaps Teebo's backside!

TEEDO

BARBAROUS JAKKU SCAVENGER

DATA FILE

AFFILIATION: None
HOMEWORLD: Jakku
SPECIES: Teedo
HEIGHT: 1.24m (4ft 1in)
APPEARANCES: VII
SEE ALSO: BB-8; Rey

TEEDOS ARE SMALL, brutish scavengers that roam the Jakku wilderness, often riding atop cyborg luggabeasts. They scavenge the dunes for salvageable technology and fiercely protect their findings with a tyrannical zeal.

Goggles

Mag-pulse grenade

Catch bottle recycles bodily fluids

TEEDOS HAVE a peculiar sense of individual identity—the name Teedo seems to identify both the species as a whole and each member within it. Despite their small size, Teedos have an exaggerated sense of their ability to intimidate.

Stealing BB-8

During BB-8's wanderings past Kelvin Ravine in the Jakku wastelands, the droid is snagged in a net by a luggabeast-riding Teedo. A young human scavenger, Rey, shouts down the surly Teedo, convincing the exasperated alien to give up his quarry after he deems the little droid not worth the hassle.

Scaly skin

Sand-shoes cut from droid treads

TESSEK

DATA FILE

AFFILIATION: Jabba's court
HOMEWORLD: Mon Cala
SPECIES: Quarren
HEIGHT: 1.8m (5ft 9in)
APPEARANCES: VI
SEE ALSO: Jabba the Hutt

Hearing organs

Manipulative mouth tentacles

TESSEK IS EMPLOYED at Jabba's palace as the Hutt's accountant. But his loyalty to Jabba is a smokescreen. Behind the crime lord's back, Tessek plots to assassinate him and take over his criminal empire. But Tessek does not realize that Jabba probably knows this, too.

TESSEK is a Quarren from Mon Cala. He was involved in galactic politics until the Empire began to enslave his people. This caused Tessek to go into hiding on Tatooine, where he found use for his financial skills among the Hutt gangsters.

Moisture-retaining robe

Scheming Reputation

Tessek lives up to some of the worst qualities attributed to the Quarren by outsiders. Because of the recurrent civil wars between them and the Mon Calamari, the Quarren have gained the reputation of being untrustworthy schemers willing to take any advantage.

TIE FIGHTER PILOT

DATA FILE

AFFILIATION: Empire
SPECIES: Human
STANDARD VEHICLE:
TIE-series starfighters
APPEARANCES: RO, IV, V, VI
SEE ALSO: AT-AT pilot

Reinforced
flight helmet

Gas transfer hose

Life-support pack

TIE targeting systems and flight
controls are superior to anything
available to rebel starfighters.

TIE FIGHTER PILOTS

form an elite group
within the Imperial Navy.
These black-suited pilots are
conditioned to be entirely
dedicated to the mission and
to destroy their targets, even if
this causes their own deaths.

Vacuum g-suit

Energy-shielded fabric

FIGHTER PILOTS take
great pride in their TIE fighters, even
though the ships lack deflector shields
and hyperdrives. The product of
intense training at the Imperial
Academies, TIE pilots are taught they
are the best in the galaxy. As a result,
they are often quite arrogant.

Battle Ready

The Empire keeps TIE fighter pilots on a
constant state of alert so they are ready for
battle at any time. Each pilot wears
reinforced flight helmets, with breather tubes
connected to a life-support pack. When in
space, they rely on their self-contained
flight suits to stay alive in their ships.

TION MEDON

PORT ADMINISTRATOR OF PAU CITY

DATA FILE

AFFILIATION: Republic
HOMEWORLD: Utapau
SPECIES: Pau'an
HEIGHT: 2.06m (6ft 8in)
APPEARANCES: III

Gray, furrowed skin from lack of light in sinkholes

Wide belt supports bony frame

Port master's walking stick

TION MEDON

is a descendent of Timon Medon, who unified Utapau. Like all Pau'ans, Tion prefers darkness to sunlight and raw meat to cooked.

Floor-length robes are a recent fashion

Utapau's surface is windswept and barren. The Utai and Pau'ans live in cities within huge sinkholes.

TION MEDON IS master of Port Administration for Pau City on Utapau. MagnaGuards kill his committee members and the Separatist leadership use his world as a temporary sanctuary.

Under Pressure

When Jedi Obi-Wan Kenobi lands at Pau City on Utapau, Tion Medon reassures the Jedi that nothing strange has happened. While Kenobi's ship is refueled, Tion whispers that Separatists have taken control of Utapau.

TOBIAS BECKETT

PROFESSIONAL THIEF

DATA FILE

AFFILIATION: His own crew, Crimson Dawn
HOMEWORLD: Glee Anselm
SPECIES: Human
HEIGHT: 1.78m (5ft 8in)
APPEARANCES: S
SEE ALSO: Han Solo; Rio Durant; Val

TOBIAS BECKETT is always scheming. He works with his crew of shady characters and the crime syndicate Crimson Dawn in the hope of making his fortune. He uses his gunslinger skills to fight, steal, and scam his way through life.

Double holster carries two guns for ambidextrous Beckett

Tobias and Val look forward to a time when it will just be the two of them together.

RSKF-44 heavy blaster

Muddy Thieves

Beckett and his crew of outlaws are posing as Imperial troopers on Mimban when they meet Han Solo and Chewbacca. Beckett has plans to steal an AT-hauler from a busy airfield for use in an upcoming job.

A SEASONED

scoundrel, Beckett pulls off such ambitious heists that he needs a crew to help him, but he never lets his guard down with them. His motto is: assume everyone will betray you and you'll never be disappointed. This is also good advice for anyone who knows him.

TUSKEN RAIDER

FIERCE TATOOINIAN NOMADS

DATA FILE

AFFILIATION: None
HOMEWORLD: Tatooine
SPECIES: Tusken
HEIGHT: 1.8m (5ft 9in)
APPEARANCES: I, II, IV
SEE ALSO: Anakin Skywalker

Gaderffii stick made from scavenged metal

Eye-protection lenses

Moisture trap

Anakin Skywalker releases his vengeful fury on the Tusken encampment.

TUSKEN RAIDERS, OR

Sand People, are fierce nomads on Tatooine. They compete with human settlers for precious moisture on the desert planet, prowling remote areas, surviving where no others can. Tusken Raiders capture Anakin Skywalker's mother, Shmi, and drag her to their encampment.

Thick desert robe

SAND PEOPLE

wear heavy clothing to protect them from the planet's harsh suns. They keep their faces hidden behind head bandages. Their traditional weapon is an ax, named a gaderffii (or "gaffi") stick.

Silent Attacker

Sand People are often taller than humans, yet they blend into the landscape with unsettling ease. They sometimes scavenge or steal from the edges of settlement zones. Only the sound of the feared krayt dragon is enough to scare the Sand People away.

During an attack, Tuskens often wield stolen weapons.

TWO TUBES

TOGNATH EGGMATES AND MERCENARIES

DATA FILE

AFFILIATION: Saw
Gerrera's militia
HOMEWORLD:
Yar Togna
SPECIES: Tognath
HEIGHT: 1.9m
(6ft 2in)
APPEARANCES:
(Benthic) S, RO;
(Edrio) RO
SEE ALSO: Saw Gerrera

Exoskeleton
skull

Before joining Saw's group,
Benthic spent time as one of
Enfys Nest's Cloud-Riders.

Sniper's
monocular
scope

Cannisters of
explosives

TOUGH, RUTHLESS
mercenaries, Edrio
and Benthic serve in
Saw Gerrera's militia.
They both get called
"Two Tubes" because
of the breathing
devices they wear
in oxygen-rich
atmospheres.

PART MAMMAL

and part insect, Tognaths
have both endo- and
exoskeletons and they see
with insectoid compound
eyes. In order to operate
on a planet like Jedha, they
have cybernetic implants
to improve their hearing
and balance.

Rifle bought
on the black
market

Eggmates

Tognath start life growing in eggs
suspended in jelly. Sometimes these
eggs fuse together, creating a strong
connection between Tognath that lasts
for life. Eggmates do not necessarily
have the same parents, but their
bond is stronger than normal siblings
and can even be telepathic.

UGNAUGHT

PORCINE SPECIES ON CLOUD CITY

DATA FILE

AFFILIATION: None
HOMEWORLD: Gentes
SPECIES: Ugnaught
APPROX. HEIGHT: 1m
(3ft 3in)
APPEARANCES: V, VI
SEE ALSO: Jabba the Hutt

UGNAUGHTS WERE sold into slavery long ago from their home planet Gentes. The eccentric explorer Lord Ecclessis Figg brought in three Ugnaught tribes to help build Cloud City on Bespin. In return, he gave them the freedom of the city.

Tusks used in blood duels

Captain's stripes

AT LEAST one Ugnaught has begun a new life away from Bespin. Yoxgit made a fortune illegally selling tibanna gas to arms dealers, then jumped the planet for Tatooine, where he found work with Jabba the Hutt.

Flight gauntlets

Stocky body is efficient at working for long periods

Cloud City Workers

Ugnaught workers in the depths of Cloud City sort through discarded metal junk, where C-3PO nearly ends up after he is blasted to pieces. The species has constructed a network of humid, red-lighted work corridors and tunnels throughout the city, most of which can only be navigated by Ugnaughts.

Ugnaughts perform the often dangerous work of mining and processing tibanna gas.

Expensive tactical boots

UNKAR PLUTT

JUNK BOSS OF JAKKU

DATA FILE

AFFILIATION: None
HOMEWORLD: Unknown
SPECIES: Crolute
HEIGHT: 1.8m (5ft 9in)
APPEARANCES: VII
SEE ALSO: BB-8; Rey; Teedo

UNKAR RUNS a profitable business stealing, scavenging, and selling scrap on Jakku. He doles out slim servings of food in exchange for valuable salvage, and calls upon leg-breakers and thugs to ensure he gets the best deals.

Buoyant, gelatinous body tissue

Apron made from salvaged hull plates

UNKAR OPERATES

out of a converted cargo crawler in a large structure at Niima Outpost. He has a monopoly on food vending in the town, and scavengers are forced to barter with him, exchanging valuable salvage for dehydrated food rations.

Boots conceal flipper-like limbs

Fish Out of Water

Unkar is an aquatic Crolute, but his greed keeps him far from the oceans of his homeworld and on Jakku, where he reigns as the undisputed junk boss. The scavenger named Rey is one of his favorite traders. When she disappoints him by backing out of a deal, Unkar takes it badly, and sends his goons to teach her a lesson.

VAL

WEAPONS EXPERT

DATA FILE

AFFILIATION: Tobias Beckett's crew, Crimson Dawn
HOMEWORLD: Unknown
SPECIES: Human
HEIGHT: 1.57m (5ft 2in)
APPEARANCES: S
SEE ALSO: Tobias Beckett; Rio Durant

During a failed attempt to secure coaxium, Val sacrifices herself in the explosion on Vandor.

A LONGTIME member of Tobias Beckett's criminal crew, Val has survived many risky ventures. She is a tough, no-nonsense weapons expert and an ace shot with a blaster rifle.

Cables carry a current that jams signal detectors

Climbing gloves have an electro-magnetic grip

VAL IS VERY

secretive about her past. Practically all anyone knows is that her father was a musician who named her after the Valachord instrument. Val is in love with Tobias Beckett, but she does not even share her secrets with him.

Syntherope for climbing

Crack Bomb Maker

Val uses her knowledge of chemistry and electronics to create explosives. For the coaxium heist on Vandor, she makes a baradium bomb to blow up the conveyex transport. The detonator is keyed to her biological signature so only she can set it off.

VICE ADMIRAL HOLDO

NOBLE RESISTANCE COMMANDER

Dyed hair is part of
her unique style

VICE ADMIRAL Amilyn Holdo
is a longtime friend and
comrade of Leia Organa's.
When Leia is injured, Holdo
takes command of her MC85
Star Cruiser, the *Raddus*. It is
one of only three remaining
Resistance ships.

Gatalentan-style
draped gown

Gatalentan bracelets

Defender-5
sporting blaster

HOLDO carries with
her the independent and
offbeat spirit of her home
planet, Gatalenta. She wears
her own style of clothes
rather than following military
uniform. Meditation and
astrology bring a calmness
to her military strategy. Her
ultimate sacrifice enables
the few remaining fighters
to escape. Thanks to her,
the spark of hope lives on.

Unassuming Hero

Holdo is an astute, levelheaded
commander, but her secretive
manner leads to some tension.
Poe Dameron even attempts a
mutiny. Modest and dedicated,
Holdo is more interested in
protecting the Resistance than
appearing a hero. And when
she sacrifices herself, Poe sees
her for the hero that she is.

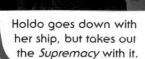

Holdo goes down with
her ship, but takes out
the *Supremacy* with it.

VOBER DAND

RESISTANCE GROUND CONTROLLER

DATA FILE

AFFILIATION: Resistance
HOMEWORLD: Suntilla
SPECIES: Tarsunt
HEIGHT: 1.73m (5ft 7 in)
APPEARANCES: VII, VIII
SEE ALSO: Nien Nunb;
PZ-4CO

Comlink headset

GLD controller's coat

STAYING EVER mobile and out of reach of First Order reprisals, the Resistance uses forgotten bases that were originally built as rebel outposts during the Galactic Civil War. These old, austere facilities ask much from the Resistance's hard-pressed ground personnel.

DURING THE Starkiller crisis, Vober Dand manages the ground crews that maintain the fleet of X-wings at the D'Qar outpost. The hard-nosed Tarsunt runs a tight operation, demanding the best of his teams of mechanics and support staff. Though it's the pilots who get the glory, Dand knows they would be grounded if not for his efforts.

Logistics Chief

In the loose-knit Resistance organization, Vober Dand holds the rank of chief of Ground Logistics Division. He is one of the first Resistance members consulted when establishing a new base, using his mathematical mind to calculate the specifics of flight schedules, maintenance requirements, and hangar operations.

Without the deep finances and government supplies of the New Republic, Vober Dand must keep the Resistance's small fleet of X-wings flying at all hours.

WAT TAMBOR

EMIR AND FOREMAN OF THE TECHNO UNION

DATA FILE

AFFILIATION: Techno Union, Separatists
HOMEWORLD: Skako
SPECIES: Skakoan
HEIGHT: 1.93m (6ft 3in)
APPEARANCES: II, III
SEE ALSO: Boba Fett; Darth Vader

Darth Vader shows no mercy to Wat Tambor on Mustafar.

Vocabulator/annunciator

Rich outer tunic over pressure suit

Dials control vocabulator

WAT TAMBOR IS FOREMAN of the Techno Union, a powerful commercial body that makes massive profits from new technologies. He is also an executive of arms manufacturer, Baktoid Armor Workshop.

TAMBOR LEFT his home planet Skako at an early age and began a career in technology on the harsh industrial world of Metalorn. Few Skakoans leave their world due to its unique atmospheric pressure. In fact, Tambor must wear a special suit to avoid his body exploding in standard, oxygen-based atmospheres.

Raiding Ryloth

During the Clone Wars, Tambor oversees the sacking of Ryloth, homeworld of the Twi'leks. Tambor and his droid army hold the capital city, Lessu, until they are pushed out during a counterattack by General Mace Windu. Tambor is then captured and imprisoned.

WATTO

TOYDARIAN JUNK DEALER

DATA FILE

AFFILIATION: None
HOMEWORLD: Toydaria
SPECIES: Toydarian
HEIGHT: 1.37m (4ft 5in)
APPEARANCES: I, II
SEE ALSO: Anakin Skywalker;
Qui-Gon Jinn; Shmi
Skywalker

WATTO IS A QUICK-WITTED, flying Toydarian shopkeeper who owns a spare parts business in Mos Eisley on Tatooine. He has a sharp eye for a bargain and spends his proceeds at podraces, gambling with Hutts, and winning slaves— including Anakin and Shmi Skywalker.

Flexible, trunk-like nose

Three-day stubble

Watto insists his shop is a parts dealership, though most would call it a junk shop.

WATTO was a soldier on his homeworld Toydaria, but left the planet after suffering an injury. On Tatooine, he watched how the Jawas sold used goods, learning some of their tricks before setting up his own business.

Large belly mostly composed of gas

Keycodes for main safe and slave keepers

Watto is surprised that his former slave, Anakin Skywalker, is now a Jedi.

Chance Meeting

When Watto meets an offworlder looking for spare hyperdrive parts, he sees an opportunity for some profitable swindling. Jedi Qui-Gon Jinn does not suspect that he will meet the prophesied Chosen One, Anakin Skywalker, in this very shop. Losing Anakin to the Jedi is the start of a downward spiral for Watto, who eventually loses his other slave, Shmi, too.

WICKET W. WARRICK

YOUNG EWOK LONER

DATA FILE

AFFILIATION: Bright Tree Village

HOMEWORLD: Forest moon of Endor

SPECIES: Ewok

HEIGHT: 80cm (2ft 7in)

APPEARANCES: VI

SEE ALSO: Chief Chirpa; Logray; Princess Leia; Teebo

Spear

Hood

Thick fur

Wicket's knowledge of the forest assists the rebels in their attack on the Imperial forces.

WICKET W. WARRICK

is a young Ewok with a reputation as a loner. He spends much time wandering far from his village in the forests of Endor's moon. Wicket is on one of his travels when he runs into Princess Leia Organa. He helps her to the safety of his treetop village, and soon comes to trust her.

YOUNG Wicket

had an adventurous childhood with his great friends—Teebo, Kneesaa, Paploo, and his brothers Weechee and Willy. Though Wicket respects the mystic shamanic magic employed by Logray, he does not possess the patience to practice it.

Friends?

Wicket bonds with Leia, and when her friends arrive, he argues that they should be spared any abuse. But his solitary habits leave him with a big lack of influence among the elders in Bright Tree Village.

REBEL ALLIANCE PILOTS

DATA FILE

AFFILIATION: Rebel Alliance/
Resistance
SPECIES: Human
STANDARD VEHICLE: X-wing
starfighter
APPEARANCES: RO, IV, V,
VI, VII, VIII
SEE ALSO: Luke Skywalker;
Poe Dameron

HEROIC X-WING pilots are the stuff of legend. Rebel Alliance pilots fly X-wing starfighters against the Empire. Later, when the Resistance is battling the First Order, its pilots draw on the same uniforms, call signs, and traditions.

Flight helmet with integrated comlink

IN THE EARLY days of the Rebel Alliance, X-wing pilots like Major Ralo Surrel are based on the Massassi outpost on Yavin 4. They fly T-65 X-wings in the first incarnations of the soon-to-be legendary Red, Blue, Green, and Gold Squadrons.

Life-support unit

Equipment pocket

Gear harness

Resistance X-wing pilots like Poe Dameron fly T-70 X-wings —the successor to the X-65.

Battle of Yavin

Pilots of Red Squadron such as Wedge Antilles ("Red Two"), Biggs Darklighter ("Red Three"), and Luke Skywalker ("Red Five") are crucial to the destruction of the first Death Star, and Antilles and Skywalker are the only two to survive. Antilles goes on to become the leader of Red Squadron at the Battle of Endor.

YADDLE

COMPASSIONATE JEDI MASTER

DATA FILE

AFFILIATION: Jedi
HOMEWORLD: Unknown
SPECIES: Unknown
HEIGHT: 61cm (2ft)
APPEARANCES: 1
SEE ALSO: Oppo Rancisis;
Yoda

SITTING ON THE Jedi High Council, Master Yaddle offers few words but much compassion and balanced patience. She looks up to Master Yoda, who is of the same species as her but is almost twice her age (Yaddle is a mere 477 years old). Yaddle has trained many Jedi Padawans, including fellow Council member Oppo Rancisis.

Mind and Body

Yaddle has devoted a lot of time to scholarly interests, and spends much time in the Jedi Archives. But she has been an active Jedi in the field, too.

YADDLE is one of the few Jedi permitted to practice morichro. This ancient art enables the user to rapidly slow down an opponent's bodily functions to the point of death.

Youthful topknot

Shapely ears

YARAEL POOF

QUERMIAN JEDI MASTER

DATA FILE

AFFILIATION: Jedi
HOMEWORLD: Quermia
SPECIES: Quermian
HEIGHT: 2.64m (8ft 7in)
APPEARANCES: 1
SEE ALSO: Obi-Wan Kenobi;
Qui-Gon Jinn

Extended neck

Traditional Quermian cannom collar

JEDI MASTER Yarael Poof is a member of the High Council at the time of the Naboo Crisis. He is a master of specialized Jedi mind tricks, which he can use to bring conflicts to a decisive end.

Deceptive Appearances

Yarael Poof quietly watches the proceedings as Qui-Gon Jinn and Obi-Wan Kenobi report from their mission to Naboo. Though appearing as a serene thinker among the Jedi Council members, Master Yarael is a dexterous combatant with a lightsaber, and has perfected many incredible moves that only his spineless anatomy can allow.

Poof has a mischievous side and enjoys playing mind tricks on colleagues.

QUERMIANS have extended necks and long limbs, as well as a second pair of arms, which Poof hides under his Jedi robe. The species is noseless, as Quermians smell with olfactory glands in their hands. They also have two brains—an upper brain in the head and a lower brain in the chest.

Robe hides second pair of arms and chest with lower brain

YODA

LEGENDARY JEDI MASTER

DATA FILE

AFFILIATION: Jedi
HOMEWORLD: Unknown
SPECIES: Unknown
HEIGHT: 66cm (2ft 2in)
APPEARANCES: I, II, III, V, VI, VIII
SEE ALSO: Luke Skywalker

Head has been nearly bald for centuries

Homespun robe

YODA IS ONE OF THE most powerful Jedi ever, and has lived to be nearly 900 years old. He served the Galactic Republic at its height, as well as through its decline and fall. Yoda is one of the few Jedi to survive the Clone Wars—he goes into hiding on the remote planet Dagobah.

Sith Fury

Accepting finally that the Clone Wars have been nothing more than a manipulation by the Sith to destroy the Jedi Order, Yoda confronts Palpatine. Even the diminutive Jedi's amazing strength and speed, however, are not a match for the devastating fury of a Sith Lord.

YODA HAS

guided hundreds of Jedi to knighthood and visited countless worlds. He takes quiet satisfaction in his ability to resolve conflict by nonviolent means, until the re-emergence of the dark side unseats others' confidence in him.

On Dagobah, Yoda trains Luke Skywalker, his final student and the galaxy's last hope.

Anakin, Yoda, and Obi-Wan Kenobi become one with the Force after their deaths.

ZAM WESELL

SHAPE-CHANGING ASSASSIN

KYD-21 blaster

ZAM WESELL is a hired assassin with a special edge. As a Clawdite shape-shifter, Wesell can change her appearance to mimic that of other species. For some years, Zam has worked with renowned bounty hunter Jango Fett.

Bodysuit stretches to allow shape-shifting

Direct-to-lungs breathpack

Blast-energy skirt

ZAM WESELL

was born on Zolan, the home of the Mabari, an ancient order of warrior-knights. The Mabari trained Zam until her desire for wealth took her to the vast metropolis of Denon, where she employed her skills and training as an assassin.

Airspeeder Chase

Zam Wesell often steals a new vehicle for each job, to avoid being traced. But she uses her own airspeeder when she knows she needs to get away fast. When Zam takes on a job for Jango Fett—to kill Senator Padmé Amidala—she has to outrun two Jedi Knights in a borrowed speeder who are hard on her trail.

Boots accept a variety of limb forms

In her true Clawdite form, Zam Wesell is a reptilian humanoid.

ZUCKUSS

GAND BOUNTY HUNTER

DATA FILE

AFFILIATION: Bounty hunter
HOMEWORLD: Gand
SPECIES: Gand
HEIGHT: 1.5m (4ft 9in)
APPEARANCES: V
SEE ALSO: 4-LOM

Compound eyes

Ammonia respirator

Heavy battle armor under robe

Breather packs

Findsman body cloak

ZUCKUSS IS an insectoid Gand bounty hunter who often partners with droid bounty hunter 4-LOM. Zuckuss is a tireless tracker, who uses the mystic findsman traditions that date back centuries on his fog-shrouded homeworld, Gand.

ZUCKUSS breathes only ammonia, so he wears a respirator in oxygen-based atmospheres. When his planet's findsman traditions began dying out, Zuckuss became one of the first findsmen to go offworld. Bounty hunting is now a lucrative way for him to use his particular talents.

Zuckuss is renowned for his tracking skills and is a highly sought-after bounty hunter.

Powerful Pair

Zuckuss's uncanny abilities make other bounty hunters uneasy. But not 4-LOM, whom Zuckuss partners with many times. The two bounty hunters make a formidable team. The pairing does not go unnoticed by Darth Vader, who hires them to locate the *Millennium Falcon*.

INDEX

ACKNOWLEDGMENTS

Penguin Random House

Senior Editor Tori Kosara
Project Editor David Fentiman
Editors Jo Casey, Matt Jones, Lauren Nesworthy, Arushi Vats
Editorial Coordinator Clare Millar
Project Art Editor Owen Bennett
Assistant Art Editor Akansha Jain
Designers Chris Gould, Jon Hall
Senior Designers David McDonald,
Mark Penfound, Clive Savage
Additional Design Sandra Perry, Dan Bunyan,
Rhys Thomas, Toby Truphet, Lynne Moulding
Pre-Production Producer Kavita Varma
Senior Producer Jonathan Wakeham
Managing Editors Sarah Harland, Sadie Smith,
Chitra Subramanyam
Managing Art Editors Neha Ahuja, Guy Harvey, Ron Stobbart
Art Director Lisa Lanzarini
Publisher Julie Ferris
Publishing Director Simon Beecroft

For Lucasfilm
Senior Editor Brett Rector
Creative Director Michael Siglain
Art Director Troy Alders
Story Group Pablo Hidalgo, Leland Chee
Asset Management Tim Map, Bryce Pinkos, Erik Sanchez,
Nicole Lacoursiere, Kelly Jensen

DK would like to thank Elizabeth Dowsett, Lisa Sodeau,
Vanessa Bird, and Vicky Armstrong for their contributions to this book.

First American Edition, 2011
This updated edition published in the United States in 2019 by
DK Publishing, 1450 Broadway, Suite 801,
New York, New York 10018

Page Design Copyright © 2019 Dorling Kindersley Limited
DK, a Division of Penguin Random House LLC
19 20 21 22 23 10 9 8 7 6 5 4 3 2 1
002-314588-Sept/2019

© & TM 2019 LUCASFILM LTD.

A catalog record for this book is available from the Library of Congress.
ISBN: 978-1-4654-8530-4

DK books are available at special discounts when purchased in bulk for sales
promotions, premiums, fund-raising, or educational use. For details, contact:
DK Publishing Special Markets, 1450 Broadway, Suite 801, New York, NY 10018
SpecialSales@dk.com

Printed and bound in China

www.dk.com
www.starwars.com

A WORLD OF IDEAS:
SEE ALL THERE IS TO KNOW